THE SIEGE OF DELHI

By the same author

THE DECADE OF REFORM: THE 1830s

THE SIEGE OF DELHI

Alexander Llewellyn

MACDONALD AND JANE'S · LONDON

For Roessa

First published in Great Britain in 1977 by
Macdonald and Jane's Publishers Ltd.
Paulton House
8 Shepherdess Walk
London N1 7LW

ISBN 0 354 04092 8

Printed in Great Britain by
REDWOOD BURN LIMITED
Trowbridge & Esher

Contents

ILLUSTRATIONS

MAPS

Introduction

The writer Harriet Martineau called the years between 1816 and 1846 the 'thirty years' peace'. The British armies and navies were seldom engaged: there was the battle of Navarino, the brief military intervention in Portugal, a disastrous expedition to Afghanistan, the opium war with the Chinese Empire and the wars against the Sikhs – but these were on the margins of empire and involved only a small part of Britain's forces. The spirit of the generation between Waterloo and the repealing of the Corn Laws was neither military nor imperialistic. There are few soldier characters in the popular novels of the day – there is the amiable sergeant at the beginning of *Great Expectations*; there are no soldier characters in their capacity as soldiers in George Eliot, Mrs Gaskell or Disraeli.

By contrast the 1850s was a decade of war. There was the conquest of Lower Burma in 1853, the war in the Crimea, the sepoy war in India, and the war against China that ended in the capture of the palace at Peking and the destruction of the Taku forts. Both in France and Britain the spirit had changed: Louis Napoleon Bonaparte had been swept into the presidency of France after a revolution as the symbol of a reviving glory; there was a clamour in Britain for a war against Russia – conservatives like the M.P. de Lacy Evans saw the Tsar as a threat to the Raj in India, and radicals like Arthur Roebuck (also an M.P.) saw him as the autocrat who had massacred his Polish subjects in 1831.

But when the decade of wars came it found the organization, the structure and the leadership of the Queen's army little changed since the days of Waterloo. The system of purchasing commissions ensured that at Balaclava the light and heavy brigades of cavalry were commanded by elderly men with a long experience of soldiering and no experience of war. The British had had for centuries a prejudice against a standing and professional army as such. It had been thought to be a threat to a nicely balanced, mixed constitution: there were the ominous lessons of the rule of the Puritan major-generals under Cromwell, the fumbling attempts of James II to threaten parliament with his army encamped at Hounslow, and the fate of Napoleonic France, an empire created by the most professional of all artillery officers. If there were to be a standing army, therefore, it should be small, its spirit should be amateur rather than professional, and above all it should be commanded by those who had nothing to gain and all to lose from the upsetting of the constitution, many of whom had paid (and the system was approved by Wellington) a kind of caution money in the form of the price of their commission.

The two greatest of the mid-Victorian wars were agents of a change that went beyond the structure of the standing army in Britain and the Raj in India. Generals who had learnt to soldier under Wellington were blamed for the administrative, medical and tactical disasters in the Crimea, and *The Times* was only half in jest when it proposed that they be replaced by directors of the new railway companies. The American Nathaniel Hawthorne overstated the case when he said that the Crimea gave Britain 'a great impulse towards democracy'; what it did give was an impulse towards professional rather than amateur administration.

British hegemony in India originated in the privileges granted to the London East India Company on the last day of 1600. Early on, the Company established a factory at Surat; then through the next hundred years extended their activities with the acquisition of Bombay as a result of the marriage of Charles II to Catherine of Braganza, and of Calcutta by purchase from the Mogul Emperor. King William III granted the Company new privileges, and in the mid-eighteenth century, after Clive's victory at Plassey, a military supremacy was secured. Two Acts of Parliament regulated the method of government in British India: Pitt's Act of 1784, which set up a Board of Control composed of members of the Company's Court of Directors and the British Government, and the Charter Act of 1833 which recognized the imperial nature of the Company's rule. It was in accordance with this last Act that Lord William Bentinck arrived in India as Governor-General, to serve the interests not only of the Company but also the Crown. By then, what had started as a privileged trading company had become, in effect if not yet in name, an empire.

Certainly the wars in India gave Britain a great impulse towards empire. First, they made empire possible. If the Gangetic plain had been lost to the Raj and the frontier with Afghanistan had been left undefended, the Russian empire would have inevitably extended through to the Punjab; and the planet, for half a century, would have been dominated by Russia rather than Britain. In the regaining of the Gangetic plain and the securing of the north-west frontier the siege and capture of Delhi was the one crucial campaign. Second, the sepoy wars brought to Victorian England an awareness of empire, its price, its obligations and its dangers.

The movement for Indian independence produced new theories of the mutiny, attempts to portray the events of 1858 and 1859 as part of a national political uprising. There was a tendency to reduce much of the argument and speculation about the complex events of two years to a debate about who committed more atrocities, and which side, indeed, started them. There is much evidence, for instance, that the practice of 'blowing away' from guns was learnt by the British from the Indians: it was the religious significance of the practice (the shattering of the body jeopardizing the soul's immortality) that was deplored rather than its cruelty – in the whole history of capital punishment there can hardly have been a more mercifully instantaneous method. But debates about atrocities are of less moment than the abiding questions, the involvement of the civil population, the presence or absence of a spirit of nationalism among the mutineers, the existence or not of a general plan on their part before the thatch burnt at Meerut and the rebel cavalry entered Delhi across the bridge of boats.

There was, of course, a considerable amount of literature on the mutiny published in 1957, its centenary. There were analyses of Indian society on its eve, the tensions between Moslem and Hindu in the north and the part played by the civil population. There was published the judicial synoptic history by Surendra Nath Sen. He concluded that the mutiny had been what contemporaries had thought it, a revolt of a large part of the Bengal army against their officers. There was another by R. C. Majumdar, which suggested that it was a sentimental myth that the mutineers in Delhi were fighting primarily to restore a free and united national empire. Any history of the mutiny or a part of the mutiny should be concentrated on the armies, their composition, grievances and conduct, the men who enlisted in them and the men who led them.

There is a wealth of contemporary sources. Foremost among them are the works of Sir John Kaye, one of the greatest and most neglected of English nineteenth-century historians – without, perhaps, the self-assured eloquence of Macaulay or the profundity of Acton, but with an eye for detail and a sane and unerring judgement of men and motives. His knowledge was immense: he had succeeded John Stuart Mill in the Political Department of the India Office having founded the *Calcutta Review* thirteen years before. Before embarking with Colonel Malleson on his six-volume history of the mutiny he had written histories of the East India Company and of the first Afghan War.

Almost every soldier of note who served in India in the 1850s seems to have left his memoirs or letters. Life in the terrible camp behind the ridge is best described by the chaplain Rotton, who accompanied Wilson's column from Meerut to Delhi in early June. The most readable, and at times moving, accounts of the assault are in the memoirs of Captain Griffiths of the 61st of Foot and Captain Anson of the 9th Lancers. Some of the most interesting comments on the leaders are in the letters of the young Frederick Roberts, who served on Nicholson's staff after the arrival of the movable column and took part in the assault on the Red Fort. There are two detailed chronicles of daily life in the besieged city, one by Maniodin, the Indian sub-inspector of police, and the other by the interpreter Jeewan Lall. Major Charles Reid left an account of the actions of the Sirmoor battalion of Gurkhas who defended the most shelled picket on the ridge, at Hindu Rao's house.

The men who commanded came, for the most part, from the service gentry of Victorian England. The very rich and the fashionable bought their way into the better regiments of the Queen's army; they often eschewed service in India. It was the sons of the lesser squirearchy of Ireland, the lowlands of Scotland and Wales, the sons of lawyers and parsons in England, who entered, often through their own public school at the Imperial Service College and their own Sandhurst at Addiscombe, the regiments of the Honourable East India Company. Hodson was the son of a West-country parson; Nicholson was from the lesser ranks of the Anglo-Irish 'ascendancy', and so too was Robert Montgomery, the grandfather of the Field-Marshal; Baird Smith, who was married to the daughter of Thomas de Quincey, was from the 'clericy' of Scotland. It is not fanciful, perhaps, to discern a similarity between this class and the Puritan service gentry who officered the armies of Oliver Cromwell.

What made the sepoy war unique among all the wars of Victorian England was that in one sense it was a total war. Both those on the ridge and those of the King of Delhi's army defending the city of Delhi fought for a total victory. The mutineers realized, as John Nicholson put it, that the punishment for their crime was death, that the fall of Delhi might mean complete destruction for them and the city. The British fought with a ruthlessness unknown in the Crimea. At their shoulders was the spectre of the Christians murdered in the palace courtyard and the children thrown into the well at Cawnpore. They might have agreed with the dictum of Clausewitz that 'in such dangerous things as war, the worst errors are caused by a spirit of benevolence'.

I have quoted freely from Anson, Griffiths and others, for they were there and saw it all: I have merely looked at the sites on the ridge and the scars on the walls.

I should like to thank Elizabeth Llewellyn for help in typing and indexing; the staff of the India Office Library (particularly Mr Philip Dymond and Miss Alison Napier); the staff of the British Museum; the staff of the Library of the National Army Museum; the staff of the Royal United Services Institution. I am grateful also to Lieut.-Col. Colin Mitchell (Argyll and Sutherland Highlanders) for introducing me to all the resources of the R.U.S.I.; to Major-General L. O. Pugh, C.B., C.B.E., D.S.O., who first showed me the privately circulated history of the Sirmoor Battalion, which was the genesis of this book; and to Captain J. G. West, R.N., for administrative assistance in connexion with the National Army Museum.

Chapter One

MUTINY

'The General is quite satisfied.'

On the night of the 10 May, 1857, a horseman clattered over the bridge of boats that spanned the Jumna river and entered the city of Delhi by the Calcutta Gate. He was a messenger from Meerut and he carried a note for the British Commissioner, Simon Fraser. The note was given to a servant who found the Commissioner in his rooms above the Lahore Gate, sprawled in a chair asleep, for he had dined well. Fraser was a man of swift temper and the servant was in two minds about disturbing him. Fraser was woken, grunted, took the note, put it in his trousers pocket and went to sleep again. He was not to open it until dawn broke, and by midday he and many of his compatriots in the ancient capital of the Moguls would be dead.

For the past months, over the cantonments, the permanent garrisons of northern India, the clouds of war had gathered. It had been decided to replace the old 'Brown Bess' that had served for a long time as the musket of the sepoys and most of the British regiments of India by a new grooved rifle. Technically the new weapon was a great improvement in accuracy, velocity and stopping power. But the new weapon needed new ammunition. Orders were in existence as early as 1847 which governed the preparation of the charges – a patch of greased calico was to cover the cartridges at one end, and this was to be bitten off before loading. Directions, too, were given about the recipe for making the grease: 'to three pints of country

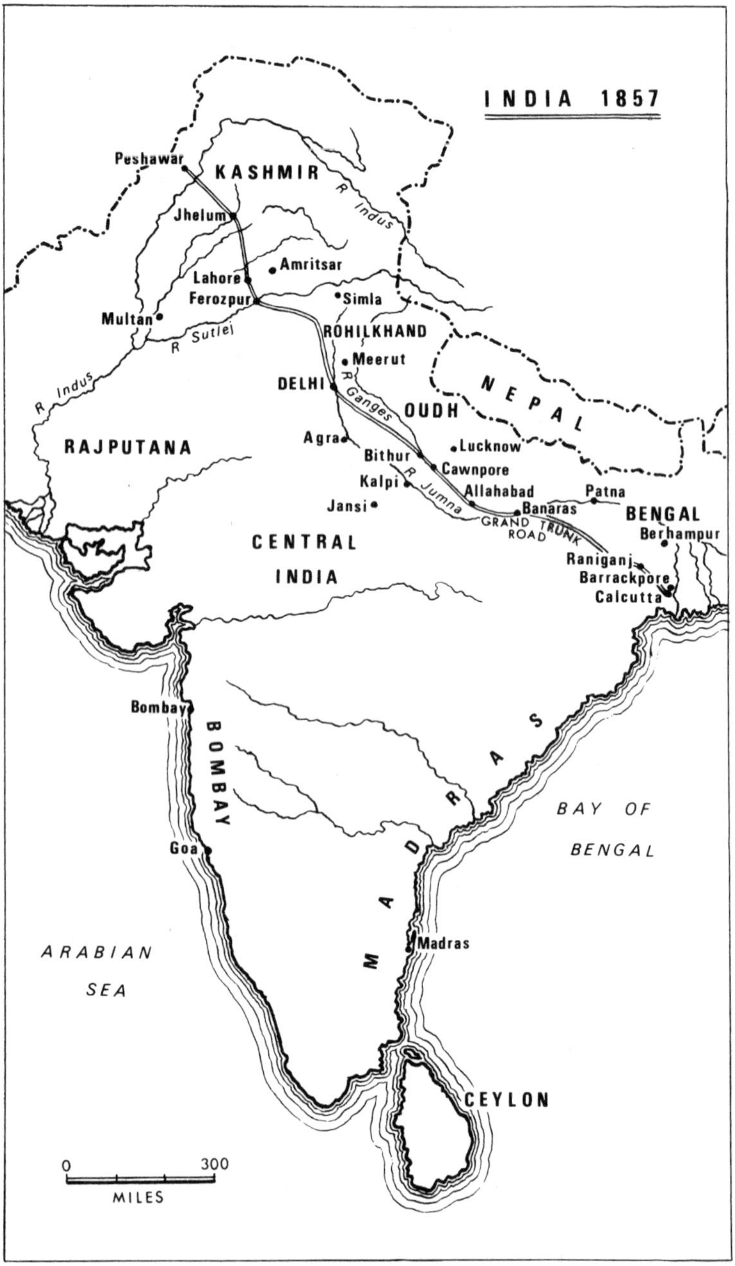
INDIA 1857
Peshawar
KASHMIR
R Indus
Jhelum
Amritsar
Lahore
Ferozpur
Simla
Multan
R Sutlej
ROHILKHAND
Meerut
R Indus
DELHI
R Ganges
OUDH
NEPAL
RAJPUTANA
Agra
Lucknow
Bithur
Cawnpore
Kalpi
R Jumna
Allahabad
Patna
Jansi
Banaras
BENGAL
GRAND TRUNK ROAD
Berhampur
CENTRAL INDIA
Raniganj
Barrackpore
Calcutta
Bombay
BOMBAY
MADRAS
BAY OF BENGAL
Goa
Madras
ARABIAN SEA
CEYLON
0
300
MILES

linseed oil, add one-fourth of a pound of beeswax, which mix by melting the wax in a ladle . . .' This would cover three yards of cloth, enough to make twelve hundred patches for cartridges.

There was nothing offensive to Hindus or Moslems in linseed oil or beeswax. But other lubricants had been used. In 1853 boxes of greased cartridges had been sent to India, not for use but for experiment, to discover what effect the climate would have on them. The lubricating agent was tallow, and some of this contained mutton-fat. One officer saw a potential danger in all this. He was Colonel Henry Tucker, then adjutant-general – that is, staff officer in charge of equipment – of the Bengal army. He sent a memorandum to the Military Board in which he suggested that 'unless it be known that the grease employed in these cartridges is not of a nature to offend or interfere with the prejudices of caste, it will be expedient not to issue them for test to Native corps, but to European soldiers only to be carried in pouch.'

Tucker's warning was never communicated by the Board to the commander-in-chief, nor was it complied with. Sepoys at Cawnpore were issued with the new ammunition: they did not use it, but, according to the original intention, carried it in their pouches and handled it in the normal course of routine. The cartridges were later returned to England with a report on their condition. There is no mention of the sepoys objecting to them, and no European regimental officer seems to have reported that they were an embarrassment. It was true, however, that cartridges greased with an obnoxious fat had been manaufactured at Cawnpore and Meerut, and that these had been dispatched to the great arsenals at Amballa and Sialkot in October 1856, but they were to be for the use not of sepoys but European troops.

But in the new year of 1857 an event took place at the arsenal of Dum-Dum near Calcutta. A lascar, an untouchable, asked to drink from the water-bowl of a brahmin sepoy and was curtly told by the brahmin that he was not prepared to lose caste. The lascar replied with the taunt that soon high and low caste would be as one, that the government was preparing new cartridges in their depots, and that Moslem and Hindu would soon be forced to bite the fat of pigs and cows. The taunt was to set the towns of northern India ablaze.

The myth – for it was nothing more – that cartridges were being greased with matter that would take away the caste of the Hindu and the soul of the Moslem was only the occasion of the sepoy revolt: the causes lay deeper, in changes of direction of the British Raj and the nature of the sepoy army. Through the early 1850s the Governor-General was Lord Dalhousie, in whom were blended the relentless logic of a Scot and the self-assurance of a liberal, utilitarian administrator. Under him the boundaries of empire had been extended, to the north-west to include the Punjab and to the east to include the coast of Burma. This was by war. But the lawyer was to complete what the soldier had started. If a rajah were to die without a son of his own, or an heir legally and publicly adopted, Dalhousie held that the state had 'lapsed' to the East India Company. Thus Sattarah, Jhansi and Nagpur were ceded to the Raj.

The final achievement of Dalhousie was the absorption of the kingdom of Oudh in 1856, a kingdom the size of Scotland that straddled the Ganges and lay on the route between the old capital of the Moguls at Delhi and the new capital of the British 'paramount power' at Calcutta. The Oudh court and government at Lucknow had been for half a century a byword for corruption, vice and cruelty. 'Everyone,' wrote Sir John Kaye, 'had his price. Place, honour, justice – everything was to be bought. Fiddlers and bankers, pimps and mountebanks, became great functionaries. There were high revels at the capital, whilst, in the interior or the country, every kind of enormity was being exercised to wring from the helpless people the money which supplied the indulgences of the Court.' British Residents, the official representatives of the 'paramount power', remonstrated at Lucknow and Governors-General protested. By a treaty of 1801 the kings of Oudh were obliged to maintain a stable and equitable rule. In 1835 the kingdom was threatened with annexation for violation of the conditions of the treaty, and in 1847 King Wajid Ali was again warned by the Governor-General, and in effect given a period of grace in which to initiate reforms.

But the urgings of the British administrators were of no avail. The King progressed from the pleasures of the bottle and dancing girls to ones less reprehensible but more childish: hours were spent in the composition of ditties, and the King would walk through the crowded bazaars of his capital banging on a drum with the rapture of a four-year-old. The British Resident at Lucknow was Colonel Sleeman, a man of long experience and a generous sympathy with India and her customs. Of all the Company's officers who had been seconded for civil duties, William Sleeman's reputation and achievement stood highest. Abstemious, a reader of the rationalist philosophers and fluent in Arabic, Persian and Urdu, he has been described as a soldier of 'Cromwellian integrity'. In the 1830s he was commissioned to extirpate the Thugs, marauding bands of ritual murderers, in Central India; and so with under a hundred soldiers and an area twice the size of the British Isles to cover, he set out to destroy what he termed 'the most dreadful and extraordinary secret society in the history of the human race'. In the process he had learnt more than any of his contemporaries about the country he served, and it was with breadth and depth of vision that he reported on the Kingdom of Oudh. He was not able to supply the Governor-General with a favourable report on the King: 'I do not think,' he wrote, 'that his majesty can ever be brought to feel the responsibilities of sovereignty strongly enough to be induced to bear that portion of the burden of its duties that must necessarily devolve upon him; he will always confide it to worthless minions who are kept for his amusement, and enjoy exclusively his society and his confidence.'

Colonel Sleeman's report had revealed a state of affairs unparallelled in any Indian principality. He had toured Oudh in 1849 and 1850, and wherever he travelled he noted in his diary examples of rapacity and lawlessness. It was the talukdars, or landowners, who kept the kingdom in a state of turbulence: 'they take to indiscriminate plunder and murder . . . no road, town, village or hamlet is safe from their merciless attacks.' But Sleeman did not recommend annexation: this policy, he wrote with foresight, would make the Raj too dependent on native armies, and 'accidents might occur to unite them . . . in some desperate act.'

In the autumn of 1854 Sleeman, soon to die, was replaced as Resident at Lucknow by James Outram who was told to make another report to the Governor-General. This he did in the following year and sent it to be digested by Dalhousie, who was in the clean bracing air of the Nilgiri Hills in the south. Outram agreed with Sleeman that annexation of the kingdom would 'tend to accelerate the crisis which the doctrines of the absorbing school must sooner or later bring upon us.' But the Governor-General took a different view, that the kingdom should be administered by the British, and its surplus revenues should accrue not to the kingdom but to the Company. This received the sanction of the Directors of the Honourable East India Company, the Board of Control for India, and the British cabinet. In January 1856 Dalhousie was told to proceed with the annexation.

In anticipation of all this arrangements had already been made: a new treaty and proclamation to the people of Oudh had been drafted, Outram had been given his instructions, even lists of administrators for the kingdom had been drawn up. By the end of the month a large body of British troops had been moved to the outskirts of Lucknow, and early in February the King agreed to receive the Resident. The audience was bizarre. The guns at the palace had been unlimbered and no salute boomed forth, nor did the sentries present arms to the representative of the 'paramount power'. Outram, accompanied by two officers, gave the King the letter from the Governor-General announcing his virtual dethronement, whereupon Wajid Ali Shah broke into clamorous grief, placed his turban in Outram's hands, refused to sign the new treaty and begged permission to go to England to plead with Queen Victoria.

A great prize had fallen to the Raj, but it was a prize to be paid for dearly. Soon the narrow, jasmine-scented streets of Wajid Ali's capital would be filled with the former soldiers of the King's army, now disbanded. One Indian, the Delhi police officer Maniodin, saw in the annexation of Oudh an immediate cause of the mutiny. 'The very bread,' he wrote, 'had been torn out of the mouths of men who knew no other profession than that of the sword.'

It was not only the princes who felt threatened by the Raj: it was also the 'talukdars', the landowners whose title to their holdings depended upon a service given to the government, the collection of taxes. Many of them were extortionate, some outrageously so, as they had been in Oudh. It was the policy of some of the new administrators, those influenced by the doctrines of Bentham and Macaulay, to obliterate this class and to place the peasant in direct relation to the civil service for the purpose of tax-collection. A settlement of the north-west provinces had started in the 1830s, and it was carried out with zeal by some of the younger administrators. 'To oust a talukdar,' wrote Sir John Kaye, 'was held by some young Settlement officers to be as great an achievement as to shoot a tiger, with just as clear a conviction of the benefit conferred upon the district in which the animal prowled and marauded.' As with the policy of 'lapse' there was opposition to the dispossession of the talukdars by some of the most experienced officials of the Raj – Robertson and Clark, two lieutenant-governors, thought it unwise; and as early as 1832 one of the Court of Directors of the East India Company itself had written that 'if an enemy appear on our Western Frontier, or if an insurrection unhappily takes place, we shall find these talukdars, I apprehend, in the adverse ranks . . .'

In the north-west and in Oudh the talukdars were disappearing: in Bengal it was those who held rent-free tenures. Rent-free holders had been called upon to register their claims in a kind of Domesday survey of 1793, and the 'permanent settlement' which resulted was looked upon as the Magna Carta of the gentry. There was resentment, therefore, in Bengal, Bihar and Orissa when in the late 1830s and and early 1840s revenue officers began to scrutinize the claims, to deplore the amount of land not subject to taxation and to treat the landowners as sinecurists living at the expense of the government and the peasantry. A policy of 'resumption' was initiated, and this spread later to the Mahratta provinces, when, in 1852, the Inam Commission, composed for the most part of army officers unversed in the law, was set up to enquire into the titles of the Mahratta landowners. Written proofs of tenure seldom existed: for the landlords generations of undisputed possession were titles enough. But the Inam Commission set about its work with zeal. The commissioners toured from village to village, and, wrote an officer who opposed this expropriation, 'each day produced its list of victims; and the good fortune of those who escaped but added to the pangs of the crowd who came forth from the shearing-house, shorn to the skin, unable to work, ashamed to beg, condemned to penury.'

Landlords were often, too, at the mercy of the civil courts and their estates sold for the recovery of trifling debts. It was as if, wrote an official, 'an English grocer, getting a decree in a small-debt court against a squire for half-a-sovereign, put up his estate in Cheshire for the same, instead of realizing the debt by the sale of his silk umbrella.'

Principalities were falling; the powers of the gentry were being eroded; above all, by the mid-century, new forces were challenging the immemorial ascendancy of the Brahmins in Hindu India. The Evangelical missionary had been in India for half a century, educating and converting. Evangelicalism and Benthamism were united in Macaulay's schemes for educational reform, which aimed at spreading knowledge of the language, institutions and religion of the mother country. The author of the *History of England* was dismayed to find Indian historiography full of kings fifty feet tall and Hindu geography full of seas of treacle. Whig history should be less mythical, if less picturesque; it should be the mentor of a new India whose guiding principle was the principle of utility. 'No Hindu,' he wrote, 'who has received an English education ever remains sincerely attached to his religion.'

It was no wonder, then, that by April of the year of storms, many sepoys feared that a greasy patch of calico might be the talisman that would charm away their heritage.

Over a quarter of a million troops were serving in India on the eve of the mutiny, in the great arsenals at Amballa, Sialkot and Dum-Dum, in the garrison towns of Barrackpore and Meerut, in the sultry cities of the Ganges plain, in the hill city of Simla (already a refuge for the government during the hottest months), in the Dravidian south and in the newly-occupied Punjab in the north-west. Of these troops less than a tenth were in the Queen's regiments, that is, British soldiers stationed in India; over two hundred and thirty thousand were sepoys in the service of the East India Company. The Company's army was divided into the forces of Madras, Bombay and Bengal. The army of Bengal garrisoned the north, the Gangetic plains, the capital of the Raj at Calcutta, the new acquisitions in the Punjab and up to the frontier with Afghanistan. It was this army that mutinied.

In many ways the sepoy army was more professional and its officers better trained than those of the regiments of the Crown. 'The regiment, in those days, was the officer's home,' wrote one of them, 'whether in camp, cantonment, or on the line of march. There was but little looking beyond, little hankering to leave it. To interest himself in the daily concerns of the sepoys, to converse with them off parade, to enter into their feelings, to contribute to their comforts, were duties, the performance of which occupied his time, amused his mind, and yielded as much happiness to himself as it imparted to others.'

That was doubtless true of the early years of the century – though even then there were occasional mutinies, as at

Vellore in the south. But by the middle of the century much of the spirit had changed. Communications with England had become easier, and by the time the new Queen came to the throne, the wives of British officers were beginning to appear in the cantonments of India. Officers previously had consoled themselves with the pleasures of the zenana which, strangely, brought benefits to their regiments; they were able the more easily to understand the sensitivities of the men by consorting with their women. But the arrival of European ladies put an end to much of the social intercourse as it did to the sexual, and by the time the reformer Bentinck became Governor-General in the 1830s there were barriers between officer and sepoy unknown in the days of Clive and Hastings.

The margin of empire, too, was extending, and this presented British officers with more sophisticated tasks. There were surveys to be made, members to be found for new commissions, duties of political representation in the native states, and for these the Company's 'civilians' were too few. Not only was there a widening gulf between sepoy and European officer, but too many of the best officers were being removed from their regiments for service on the staff or as civil administrators. At the same time the powers of the commanding officers were being reduced: they were no longer to have a final say in promotions, rewards and punishments. All this was reinforced in a General Order of 1824; each native infantry regiment was to be divided into two battalions, and the officers to be distributed between them without regard to past associations and attachments.

Not only did the reformers centralize; they also, misguidedly, tried to humanize, and under Bentinck flogging as a punishment was abolished. There was opposition to this, mainly from the Indian officers, all of whom had risen from the ranks. Thomas Seaton, a colonel of great experience, wrote that the abolition was almost universally condemned by them. Another commanding officer took soundings among his native officers, and their verdict was unanimous: 'If you abolish flogging, the army will no longer fear, and there will be a mutiny.'

Even before these reforms there had been mutinies in the sepoy regiments. In 1806 the Madras army had been ordered to remove caste-marks and ear-rings, and to wear a leather cockade made from the hide of pigs or cattle. These orders came at an unfortunate time, when there was a rumour that native troops in Ceylon had been forced to attend a Christian church parade. Sepoys had plotted a general uprising at Vellore, the murder of their officers by night and the seizure of the cantonments. All for a time was chaos: but relief came from Arcot, and the mutiny was suppressed. Retribution was thorough – some of the mutineers were shot out of hand, others reserved for the hangman's rope after court-martial. A few years later sepoys of the Bengal army refused orders to serve in Burma: to cross the sea was against the code of their caste, and there had been rumours that British troops there had been defeated and that the Raj was crumbling. The Commander-in-Chief, Sir Edward Paget, tried to disabuse the sepoys of their fears, but when they refused to march, his action was swift and terrible. A large force of British troops was moved to the garrison town of Barrackpore, and many of the sepoys were mown down with grapeshot. One regiment, the 47th, was disbanded and its name removed from the List.

Victories themselves brought embarrassments of a different kind. The sepoys' pay – indeed the pay of all soldiers, officers and men, European and Indian – was a complicated affair, eroded by deductions and supplemented by allowances. For the sepoys of the Bengal army pay was of crucial importance. The Madras army was accustomed to being accompanied by wives and families when posted: the Bengal army, many of whom were Moslems whose women were carefully protected, was not, and much of their pay had to be remitted to support their homes. When serving outside British India a special allowance was paid. But when new territories were conquered, like Sind in 1843, the allowances were stopped, as the areas had now become part of British India.

Thus in early 1844 the 34th Native Infantry halted at Ferozpur and refused to enter the newly-conquered territories unless its 'batta' (special allowances) were restored, and the spirit of mutiny spread to the 4th and the 69th. The colonel of the 64th put a gloss of his own on an ambiguous directive about pay, and read it to his regiment. Sepoys were led to expect a monthly payment of 12 rupees, and when, on reaching Shikapur, they received only 8, the pay was sullenly refused, and the regiment piled their arms. Through a June day, with the sun beating fiercely on the plain, the sepoys refused to take up their arms, return to their lines or cook or eat. Either, they demanded, the promised 'batta' be restored, or they would be discharged and return to their homes. That night the sepoys, still in their uniforms and unfed, stayed away from their lines and wandered about the camp resentfully discussing their grievances among the piles of arms.

The next day a general officer was sent to make an enquiry and to calm the regiment. Sepoy after sepoy told the same story: that the payment had been promised by their colonel, and had not been forthcoming. The colonel was at once relieved of his command, and later cashiered. Thirty-nine of the mutineers were sent for trial – one was acquitted, thirty-two were imprisoned, and six were hanged.

There was a pattern to these mutinies: they were almost an extension of bargaining rather than a deliberate disavowal of allegiance. Indeed there is evidence that the sepoys never had the notion of allegiance; loyalty to a king or a country was the culture of European soldiery since the Renaissance. The sepoy's loyalty was to the colours of his regiment, to a band of brothers at the head of whom was his colonel. His oath was not one of allegiance to a king, but an oath to be true to his 'salt', his paymaster, the Honourable East India Company. It has been pointed out that there is no word for 'mutiny' in Hindustani; the nearest to it is a word meaning 'faithlessness' or 'ingratitude'. In the literal sense a sepoy was a mercenary – his loyalty was to his fellows: he was doing a job and doing it for money; he had made a bargain and taken an oath to keep his part of it – but his paymasters, of course, must keep theirs. To refuse to serve when he considered that the paymasters' side of the bargain was not being kept, did not appear to the sepoy as the heinous military offence that his European officers considered it.

In 1849 the Commander-in-Chief in India was Sir Charles Napier. He was perhaps the shrewdest, most discerning and humane of any of the Queen's generals, especially in matters of human relationships. Ten years before in northern England he had averted a possible Chartist uprising by a combination of sympathy and firmness. Napier decided to tour the regiments of the Bengal army, and to make a report on their morale to the Governor-General. The evidence that Napier collected on his tour convinced him that no less than twenty-four regiments might mutiny and, as the question of pay seemed to him of most moment, he took a bold step. He ordered that an allowance which rose with the cost of provisions should be paid until he had received the sanction of Dalhousie, who was not at the time at the seat of government in Calcutta.

On his return Dalhousie considered that his authority had been flouted. There was an acrimonious public quarrel between the General and the Governor. Napier insisted that he was acting within the limits of his discretion and that there was the danger of a general uprising of the native regiments garrisoned in the newly-conquered provinces. The result was the resignation of the most talented officer in the service of the Company or Crown.

There was the problem, too, of caste. Many of the most experienced officers advocated a policy of recruiting exclusively from the brahmins; others advocated a mixture of castes – but in this case was not the sepoy sometimes the master of the officer? 'I cannot conceive,' wrote Major-General Birch, 'the possibility of maintaining discipline in a corps where a low-caste non-commissioned officer will, when he meets off-duty a brahmin sepoy, crouch down to him with his forehead on the ground. I have seen this done.' Were not only castes, but races, to be mixed in the same regiment? Some thought this would reduce the possibility of dangerous combinations and intrigues that might arise in regiments exclusively Pathan, or Sikh or Mahratta, and one general of long experience, Hearsey, had even suggested that the army should recruit abroad among Christians from the Middle East, Malaya, China or even Latin America ('they must be Christians, and then *Trust* can be reposed in them').

Those of high caste in the armies of Bombay and Madras were able with comparative ease to conform to the customs of the service, but they were in proportion far fewer than the brahmins in the army of Bengal. Above all this propaganda could be insidious. Was the Company trying to obliterate caste, as, it was claimed, they had attempted to do in their prisons? But, as an officer at the time noted, 'old officers would not believe that the men, along with whom they had marched and fought for a generation, in whose chivalrous honour their faith had never been shaken, and whom they loved and were proud of, could prove unfaithful to their salt. If they perceived any disaffection, it was in some other regiment than their own.'

The princes were being dethroned, the gentry evicted, and the brahmin priesthood was losing power and influence in the face of new laws and new teachings. Perhaps the structure and the very existence of the Bengal army was another attack on the ancient customs of the people?

Then, in July 1856, came an indication to the conservative and orthodox that this was indeed the case. Twice native troops had been needed for service in Burma, and on one occasion the attempt to move them had ended in mutiny. The Bay of Bengal, now a British lake, was to the sepoy the 'black water', full of evil omen: to cross it was an insult to his caste, for it was the untamed sea that led to a land defiled and full of infidels. On 25 July a General Enlistment Act was promulgated by the new Governor-General, Lord Canning: from now on the government of India would accept as recruits only those who would 'distinctly undertake to serve beyond the seas, whether within the territories of the Company or beyond them.' Canning was delighted with this edict and wrote to the

President of the India Board that at last he had put an end to the 'most impolitic, embarrassing and senseless practice of enlisting the native army of Bengal for limited service only . . .'

Some saw the General Enlistment Act as an attempt to rid the Bengal army of sepoys of a high caste, and this belief was strengthened when there was at the same time an attempt made to recruit Sikhs from the newly-conquered territories. Did this not indicate that the government had done with the old Bengal army that had existed since the days of Clive, and was prepared to create a new one, an army of mercenary coolies, prepared to serve anywhere?

There was other evidence of attacks on brahminism. The wife of the Governor-General had been visiting Christian girls' schools in Calcutta, and Lord Canning himself had sent donations to a Bible society busy translating the scriptures into the languages of India. There had appeared anonymously a Christian manifesto which declared that in the age of railways and the electric telegraph, when it was becoming evident that the highest aspirations of all men were the same, the whole sub-continent should embrace one religion, that of the masters; and one lieutenant-governor reported that many of the more intelligent Moslems were convinced that the government was 'immediately about to attempt the forcible conversion of its subjects.' In the Bengal army, too, there were proselytizing colonels. Colonel Wheler, who commanded a regiment of infantry used 'to speak to all classes, sepoys and others . . . on the subject of religion, in highways, cities, bazaars and villages.' He said that he did this out of a conviction that every Christian was bound 'to make known the glad tidings of salvation to his lost fellow-creatures', when speaking, therefore, to a native on the subject of religion, 'I am then acting in the capacity of a Christian soldier under the authority of my heavenly superior.'

By the new year of 1857 wild rumours, fanned by the resentful and the credulous, were spreading like coils of smoke through the cantonments and bazaars. The bones of cows were being ground to mix with bread at Cawnpore; the wells had been defiled at Lucknow; the prisoners in Calcutta were being forced to use eating vessels that had been defiled; the soldiers throughout the north would have to bite grease obnoxious to both Moslem and Hindu, high caste and low.

Then, at Barrackpore, a drugged and besotted sepoy challenged the authority of the army and the Raj.

His name was Mangal Pandy – and from then on 'Pandy' was to be the nickname for a mutinous sepoy used by the British soldiers.

Barrackpore was the largest garrison town in the area around Calcutta. In mid-March a mutinous regiment had been quartered there to await disbandment, and by the end of the month, with the hot weather approaching, rumours and fears bred like flies. On the morning of the 29th the British regimental sergeant-major of the 34th Native Infantry, Hewson, was summoned from his bungalow by an Indian officer. He was told that a sepoy of his regiment had run amuck, was strutting in front of the quarter-guard on the parade ground with a loaded musket and calling on his fellows to defy the army and the Raj. Hewson warned his adjutant, Lieutenant Baugh, and walked calmly to the parade ground. Mangal Pandy, his courage raised by a dose of the drug 'bang', crouched behind the station gun when he saw his sergeant-major, shot at him and missed. The adjutant arrived on his horse; Mangal Pandy fired again and hit not the rider but the horse, whereupon the adjutant rushed the mutineer who slashed him on the hand and neck with his sword. Then sergeant-major and adjutant tried to grapple with Pandy and disarm him.

The twenty sepoys of the guard, under a native officer called Issuri Pandy, stood by, unconcerned, while the three men brawled in the dust under the station gun. One man only came forward, a Mohammedan, Sheikh Pultu, and rescued Baugh and Hewson, but without capturing Pandy. By then other British officers had arrived, among them the Colonel Wheler who had written the Evangelical tracts for his regiment. It was he who ordered the quarter-guard to seize Pandy: the order was refused. The commander of the division was the courageous veteran, General Hearsey. He arrived with his two sons to witness a chaotic and humiliating scene; British officers had been threatened with rifle butts; a guard had refused the orders of a regimental commander; a subaltern and a sergeant-major had been unable to arrest a drug-crazed mutineer. A British officer shouted a warning to the general that Pandy's musket was loaded. 'Damn his musket,' Hearsey muttered, and drawing his revolver addressed the guard: 'Listen to me: the first man who refuses to march when I give the word is a dead man.' Reluctantly, following the general, the guard prepared to move on Mangal Pandy, but the wretched man saw that he had lost and, in an attempt to avert the terrible consequences of his defiance, turned his musket on himself. The young Frederick Roberts saw it all. 'There was a shot, the whistle of a bullet,' he wrote, 'and a man fell to the ground – but not the General! It was the fanatic sepoy himself, who at the last moment had discharged the contents of the musket into his own breast.' The sepoy was wounded and not killed.

On 6 April Mangal Pandy faced a court-martial composed of native officers, and two days later was hanged in front of the whole garrison. On the 10th and 11th Issuri Pandy, the Indian officer who had commanded the quarter-guard, was tried, and he, too, was sentenced to be hanged, but the execution, to the annoyance of the Governor-General, was delayed for nearly a week. A legal wrangle took place after sentence was passed on the officer: apparently Hearsey had been empowered to carry out executions on sepoys and non-commissioned officers only, and the Advocate-General, erroneously, advised that he should be given a special warrant. The delay lessened the exemplary effect of the hanging and also gave the impression of hesitancy on the part of the government: about this, Canning wrote to the India Board in London, he was 'vexed'.

Through April the disaffection spread. At the arsenal at Amballa Lieutenant Martineau, a young officer who was on excellent terms with the sepoys, was told by his men that those who handled the new cartridges were to be treated as outcasts by the orthodox. 'Good God,' he wrote angrily, 'here are all the elements of combustion at hand': many of the sepoys were 'sullen, distrustful, fierce'. It was no more than Napier had predicted seven years before and it might have been avoided if Colonel Tucker's warnings had been heeded.

General Anson, the Commander-in-Chief of the Bengal army, was firmly against concessions in the matter of handling the cartridges. Through an interpreter, he addressed the garrison at Amballa – discipline must be maintained; the routines of training continued; there had been ample proof that the cartridges were not contaminated; it was only evil propaganda by designing persons that had fixed such a notion in the minds of the sepoys. And when Major Boyd of the 2nd Bengal Fusiliers wrote to Anson that his servants had told him that there were nightly meetings of the sepoys plotting 'bad things' the general neither answered nor acknowledged his letter.

Then the burnings began. Nightly, first at Amballa then in other cantonments in the north, the bungalows of officers were set on fire. More ominous even than this, perhaps, incendiarism spread to the sepoy lines, as a warning to those who had handled the cartridges: on 27 April the first sepoy hut went up in flames, and on the following night five more.

Stories of another sort were being spread in Delhi. Here was the court of the aged titular king, the descendant of Timur and heir of the Moguls, in the ancient imperial city of Akbar and Shahjehan. At Bahadur Shah's court news of the disturbances at Barrackpore and Amballa was not unwelcome. In March a proclamation had appeared on the walls of the mosque in central Delhi, Jumma Masjid: this purported to come from the Shah of Persia and announced that an army was poised to invade India and expel the British, calling on all true Moslems to join in a 'jehad' or holy war. What was the origin of the proclamation? Although Simon Fraser had had it ripped down within hours of its first appearance, others like it began to be posted up on the public buildings of the city. The Shah had certainly tried to provoke disturbances in the Bengal army at the time of the Persian wars a few years earlier. At the same time an Indian journal claimed that Dost Mohammed of Afghanistan, in name the ally of the British, was preparing to join the Shah. Might not even the Russians join in? There were exaggerated accounts of the reversals of the Queen's soldiers in the Crimea.

Through that overcast April a disgruntled grandee was moving round the country. He was the Nana Sahib, son of the dispossessed ruler of Poona, who held court – paid for by a pension from the Company – at Bithur. For a long time he had been agitating for an increase in the pension and had even sent a representative to London on his behalf, a smooth Moslem lawyer who enjoyed high life. From Bithur the Nana Sahib travelled to Delhi, Kalpi and Lucknow. When he visited the official Martin Gubbins at the Residency in Lucknow, the Nana Sahib's manner was 'arrogant and presuming'; and he was seen parading through the city 'with a retinue more than usually large'. There were no waters more troubled for the Nana Sahib's fishing than in the capital of the annexed kingdom. Here was a long history of banditry; here were dispossessed nobility of the old order; here the government of the British was tenuous and established as many thought, with ignominy and disgrace. The Resident, Sir Henry Lawrence, had achieved much: but there were, he wrote to the Governor-General that month, 'many thousands (twenty thousand I was told . . .) of disbanded soldiers, and of hungry, nay starving, dependents of the late government' loose in the teeming bazaars.

There were the activities, too, of the Maulvi, who had toured the cities of Oudh preaching a holy war until he had been arrested and imprisoned. And chapatis began to be passed as a kind of chain letter from village to village: each recipient was told to make five more, the size of the palm of a hand, and to pass them on. Maniodin, the Delhi police officer, intercepted some, but his questionings could not uncover the message they were meant to convey. Magistrates tried to break the chain; but whatever the message was it continued to be received through the provinces of the north-west 'like the fiery cross that summoned the clansmen of Roderick to battle'.

During April the banked fires were smouldering: in May, as if there had been a puff of the bellows, they burst into flame. It all started in the cantonments of Meerut, the headquarters of a divisional area that included Delhi. The 3rd Light Cavalry was stationed here, a regiment of great distinction, one which the young Hugh Gough who had just joined it thought to be smarter than any of the Queen's regiments of cavalary. Moreover, it had always been thought that the feeling against the cartridges was mainly among the Hindus, and that the cavalry, being mostly Moslems, were particularly reliable. It was commanded by a Colonel Carmichael Smyth, of whom Sir John Kaye wrote that 'the unquestionable honesty of his nature was of that querulous, irritable cast which makes a man often uncharitable and always unpopular.' At the end of April Carmichael Smyth returned to his regiment from leave and, determined once and for all to scotch the stories of the greased cartridges, he ordered on parade the picked élite of the regiment, 'the skirmishers', ninety of them, in order to demonstrate to them a method of loading which would not involve biting the patches of calico, but simply tearing or pinching them off with the fingers. Only five on parade would accept the cartridges; eighty-five 'respectfully refused the order'.

The colonel discussed the situation with Melville Clark, the adjutant, while the parade was drawn up in the fierce morning sun. Then he dismissed the parade, and the men, chattering and tense, went back to their lines. The story spread through the bazaars and brothels of the garrison town. The British officers' bluff had been called: the eighty-five had preferred their faith to the 'salt' of the Company.

Above Sepoys at rifle practice at the time of the mutiny.
Below 'Blowing away' from the guns. It was more usual for the condemned to stand with his back to the gun.

Above left Brigadier-General John Nicholson, who led the assaulting columns on 14 September 1857. *Above right* Earl Canning, Governor-General of India at the time of the mutiny. *Below left* Bahadur Shah Zafar, King of Delhi and last of the Moguls. *Below right* Begum Zinat Mahal, wife of the King of Delhi.

Smyth, as he had to, sent a report to the commander of the division, General Hewitt, an elderly, irritable soldier, so stout that he could not mount a horse and appeared on parade in a special buggy that he had designed himself. He was the general who had been relieved of his command near the frontier at Peshawar because he was 'too inactive'. He gave the only decision that he could in the face of a deliberate refusal to obey an order: there was to be an immediate court-martial.

The court was convened on Friday, 8 May, and was composed of native officers hurriedly assembled, some from the garrison at Delhi forty miles away. The mess room of the cavalry regiment was chosen, the only available room large enough and, conveniently, one that was not roofed with thatch – there was a general fear among the British officers of incendiarism. The officers who composed the court sat behind a plain, scrubbed, trestle table, and the eighty-five – a cross-section of their regiment, thoughtful long-service sepoys among the defiant youngsters – squatted on their haunches on the ground in front of their judges.

The verdict could not have been in doubt. General Hewitt, with the irritability of an elderly man who felt that he and the Raj had been slighted, ordered a parade of the whole garrison for the passing of the sentences, which were severe. The mildest was ten years with hard labour: the harshest life sentences to be served on the remote penal camps in the Andaman Islands. So on the Saturday the garrison paraded, forming three sides of a hollow square, with the European troops – the 60th Rifles and the 6th Dragoon Guards – armed on the flanks, and the Indian regiments, without ammunition, in the centre and facing Hewitt, Brigadier Archdale Wilson and the staff.

After the sentences were read, the uniforms were stripped from the shoulders of the eighty-five; then from beyond the parade ground could be heard the clanking of chains as a contingent of armourers from the Horse Artillery arrived. The sentenced sepoys were ordered to remove their boots, and, under the scorching sun, the slow business – it was to last for several hours – of the riveting of shackles began. It was noon before the condemned were marched off, barefoot and in leg-irons. The whole of these proceedings had passed in a tense silence, but as the sentenced sepoys passed their colonel, one of them hurled his boots in the direction of the staff; another cried 'for the faith' and his cry was taken up by others. As the eighty-five men were led to gaol, Hugh Gough noticed a restlessness among the Indians on parade, a shuffling in the hot, dry dust; but the European troops, with loaded muskets, were called to attention and there was no answering gesture of defiance.

Hugh Gough was an intelligent, courageous young man – he was to rise to be a general and to be awarded the Victoria Cross – and to him fell a poignant duty. He had to attend to the prisoners in the gaol, and pay them, for the last time, the money owed to them by the Company. Men of long service, whose pensions were now forfeit, whose fathers and grandfathers had served their time in the same regiment with honour, wept and implored him to intercede ('I have seldom, if ever, in all my life experienced a more touching scene,' he wrote years later); while through the scorching afternoon and sultry evening sepoys in the lines, the bazaars and the brothels ruminated on the harshness of the sentences and the plight of the convicted.

Like rats to a garbage heap, the discontent in the garrison had drawn the 'badmashes', the bad characters, from the surrounding villages to swell the population of Meerut, and that night coils of smoke rose from burning thatch. Gough himself was warned by a havildar that the sentences were deeply resented and that on the following day, the Sunday, there would be an attempt to release the prisoners. Gough reported this to Carmichael Smyth and the brigadier, Archdale Wilson, but both shrugged it off as idle bazaar gossip. Hewitt had already written a complacent report on the whole affair which concluded that the disposition of the sepoys was excellent. 'The general,' Gough was told by Wilson, 'is quite satisfied.'

Sunday 10 May dawned with the promise of heat. Through the morning all was quiet in the garrison town. The shops were open in the bazaar. Traders haggled. Travellers were unmolested. The Europeans attended the morning service conducted in the garrison church by the Reverend James Rotton; but many of them, when they returned to their bungalows in the middle of the day, found that their servants had gone. In the early afternoon the rumour spread: at 2 o'clock a girl in the market was told that the 3rd Cavalry were going to rise and release their comrades from gaol, and at about four the electric telegraph line from Meerut to Delhi was cut. Most of the Europeans slept through the sultry afternoon, to be woken in time for the evening service when the European troops paraded and the officers' wives and the civilians again assembled at Rotton's church.

Hugh Gough was still asleep when the Indian officer who had warned him of trouble the night before arrived at his bungalow. The lines of the native regiments were on fire; the 3rd Cavalry had broken into the gaol and released their comrades. Gough was the first British officer to reach the scene. At first he tried to turn out his own troop, but they turned on him and, with a British quartermaster-sergeant, he pulled his horse round and galloped to safety through the crowded bazaar, where he had, he wrote later, literally to cut his way, pelted with stones, 'through hundreds of men armed with tulwars and lathies', [sticks used as a weapon] while the burning of bungalows and the slaughter of Europeans began. Hervey Greathed, the commissioner, was saved by his own servants: when mutinous sepoys came to the gates of his bungalow they were told he was away, while he and his wife crouched in hiding on the roof. Hearing the commotion in the lines Colonel Finnis, who commanded the 11th Native Infantry, went to remonstrate with his men, when sepoys of another regiment, the 20th, riddled him with bullets. He was the first officer to be killed.

But apart from Finnis most of the senior officers seem to have been curiously inert. Carmichael Smyth never went near the lines of his regiment from the time of the fatal parade when the cartridges were issued until the men rose during the night of the 10th; it was two junior officers of the 3rd Cavalry, Craigie and the acting adjutant, Melville Clark, who vainly attempted to quell the riot. Hewitt, elderly, irritable and indecisive, watched the fires in the lines from the verandah of his bungalow, in his pyjamas: he was the commander of the divisional area, and responsibility for what went on in the garrison, he thought, belonged to the garrison commander, Archdale Wilson. So Hewitt ordered the European troops back 'to strengthen the barracks and take precautions against attack', while from the bazaar and the villages the badmashes began a plundering of the lines that was to last all night. Soon after this the general went on sick leave and then back to England, 'protesting on the way,' wrote one of his officers, 'that if he had to manage the thing over again, he could not have done it otherwise.'

The fires and killing spread, and by nightfall the town was in the hands of the mutineers, joined by the badmashes, eager for plunder and fortified by drink and drugs. Then one of the mutineers gave the alarm: one of the Queen's regiments, the 1st Battalion of the 60th Rifles, had been issued with ammunition and was on its way to avenge the slaughtered Europeans – and the cry went up, 'Quick, brothers, quick! To Delhi! To Delhi!'

Chapter Two

DEFEAT

'If you want to stay alive, you must get out of this place.'

Dawn broke over the city of Delhi with the promise of heat. The ancient city was girded on three sides by a massive wall forty feet high, punctured on the north by the Kashmir Gate, on the west by the Lahore and Kabul Gates, and on the south by the Delhi Gate. To the east ran the river Jumna, at places over a mile broad, studded with islands and sandbanks. At its narrowest point, where the fort of Selimgarh stuck out into the river, there was a bridge of boats joining the west bank to the east, the link between Delhi and the road that led to the garrison at Meerut forty miles to the north-east. The city was bisected by the street of the silversmiths, the Chandni Chouk, that ran from the Lahore Gate to the walls of the palace; to the south of this was one of the greatest mosques of Islam, the Jumma Masjid, to the north the powder-magazine. Delhi teemed with a population of nearly three hundred thousand, about half Moslem and half Hindu.

Inside the walls lay a city within a city, part palace and part fortress, where lived the 82-year-old King with a multitude of courtiers, lawyers, doctors, poets and rhapsodists, in teeming alleys and courtyards behind the blood-red walls. This was the Red Fort, where there was 'a maze of houses, some of masonry, some of mat, some of mud', houses that contained underground rooms and secret passages, 'dark and mysterious holes and corners, secret doors and outlets.' Here the magnificence of audience hall and peacock throne were set

THE SIEGE OF DELHI

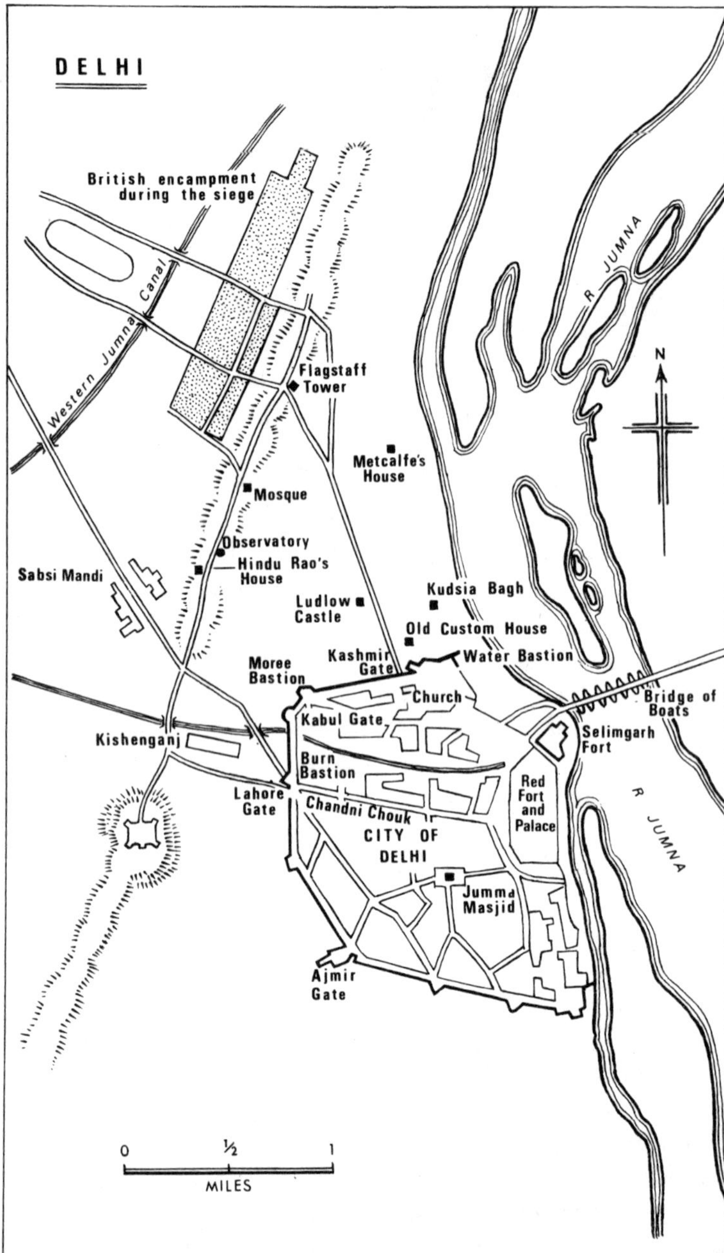

beside dirt and filth. 'Rich carpets and dirty mats were side by side on the floor; ivory and silver chairs were covered with rags.' Here hundreds of the young lived without work, the old with nothing but memories of past glory and power and little to look forward to but the grave. 'The young were given over to lust, the old to intrigue . . .'

This was all that was left of the empire of Akbar and Shahjehan, a ramshackle court like a tiny city, where, wrote a contemporary, incest, murder, poison and torture were daily occurrences; where girls gleaned from the surrounding villages 'danced naked to inflame the passion of old age'; a haven for fugitive criminals, a den of forgers, swindlers and thieves, where 'wives intrigued against wives, harlots against wives, mothers against sons.' Here assassinations were frequent and the silent river flowing past the eastern gates could keep her secrets. The palace was, as Emily Eden the traveller described it, 'a melancholy red-stone notion of life'.

Here lived Bahadur Shah, heir of the Moguls, white-bearded, sad and ruminative. He ordered a bulletin to be issued daily, chronicling the petty happenings of the decaying court. He distributed charms and talismans, and believed, we are told, that he could turn himself into a house-fly when the occasion warranted. Most of the day he spent propped on pillows, sometimes smoking his hookah, sometimes composing his Persian couplets; or, leaning on a long staff, he would shuffle to the audience hall and wearily listen to the endless pleas of his subjects, the gossip of the women and the tale-bearing of the men. As he lay against his pillows an inspiration for a couplet had come to him. It has been aptly translated:

Not Czar of Russia nor Sultan made the conquest easy,
The only weapon was a cartridge greasy.

And of this, hearing of the fires of Meerut and Barrackpore, the rumblings of Amballa, and the unease along the Gangetic plain, the King felt proud.

His position was anomalous: since the fall of Delhi to the

Raj at the beginning of the century, the administration of the city was in the hands of the British – there was the Commissioner Simon Fraser, a magistracy headed by Sir Theophilus Metcalfe and a newly appointed judge, C. T. Le Bas, who had arrived in the new year. But within the dark purlieus of the palace the old King was still an emperor. British officials approached him barefoot and with obeisance. He held court and listened to the unending petitions of his subjects in the audience hall .He was the source of favours and the leader of the faithful at prayer.

Over the years there had been lengthy and bitter arguments with the officials of the Raj. There was a complicated dispute over the succession. There was the question of the opening of the gate that led from the Selimgarh Fort – opposed by the British and demanded by the King as it would give him easier access to the Jumna on the east of the palace; the King had won. But over all there hung a sentence of death: it seemed to be British policy that with the passing of Bahadur Shah the imperial dignity itself should come to an end.

Within the city there were practically no European troops. The King had a small guard commanded by a British officer, Captain Douglas. The guard was mainly for ceremonial, of artillery and infantry. Captain Douglas' quarters were above the Lahore Gate at the westernmost part of the fortress walls.

To the north of the palace lay the great powder-magazine, an arsenal surrounded by high walls with heavy gates. General Napier had earlier pointed out the imprudence of keeping so large a store of ammunition within the centre of the city, and another had been constructed outside the walls. This arsenal was manned by three European subalterns under Lieutenant Willoughby, six European sergeants and conductors, and a body of lascars, Indian coolies. Here in the early hours of the morning of Monday, 11 May, Lieutenant Willoughby was about his duties. At a little after 8 o'clock, another of the magazine's subalterns, Lieutenant Forrest, arrived accompanied by the chief magistrate Sir Theophilus Metcalfe. They requested arms from the magazine.

Less than an hour before that the dust raised by a body of cavalry had been seen on the road to the east of Delhi. They were the mutineers of the 3rd Cavalry from Meerut. Shortly before 8 o'clock they clattered across the bridge of boats, killed the toll-keeper and an Englishman leaving the city, and were clamouring at the gates of the palace. The King was disturbed by the commotion and shuffled to the balcony on which he was used to appearing before his subjects and listening to respectful pleas for favours. But what he saw was a group of about forty sowars, Indian cavalrymen, who had entered the fortress through the Rajghat Gate that had been unbarred for them by a Moslem crowd. It was Ramadhan, the month of fast, when many Moslems in the city had tempers frayed by day-time starvation, and nerves taut from the heat and the fervour of a warlike religion. The dust rose as their horses reared, and the cry came from the Meerut mutineers: 'Help, O King! We pray for assistance in our fight for the faith!'

Blinking in the bright light and the clouds of dust, the King sent for Douglas who joined him on the balcony and first ordered, then pleaded with the sowars to disperse. But his words were drowned in a chorus of insolence. Meanwhile the guard went over to the mutineers, a small detachment went south of the city to break into the gaol and release the prisoners, and a mob of mutineers poured into the courtyards of the palace through the eastern gate.

And then the killing began.

Simon Fraser was the first to be mown down. He had made his way through the swelling crowds to Captain Douglas' quarters above the Lahore Gate of the palace, weaving his way in his buggy. He reached the steps that led to the door, leapt out, and was killed by one stroke from the sword of a lapidary.

Meanwhile Captain Douglas had escaped the crowds outside the King's balcony by jumping into the moat. He had smashed his ankle and been smuggled, semi-conscious, to his own quarters. He was given something to drink and his leg was being bandaged, when he heard a hammering on the door. It was opened to admit the Delhi chaplain, Jennings, his daughter, and an 18-year-old girl from England, Miss Clifford, who was the sister of a civil official at Agra. They had emerged to see the cause of the commotion, and now sought sanctuary. But the sanctuary was only to last for minutes. The mob rushed the stairs, cut down Douglas and Jennings, and dragged the young women from their hiding-place in a mahogany wardrobe.

Maniodin, the Indian sub-inspector of police, first heard of the disturbances when he was told by the Collector, Hutchinson, that the Calcutta Gate was to be barred, as the mutineers were streaming across the bridge of boats. As early as 9 o'clock, he reported later, 'the principal executive officers of the Government were dead. Then there ensued a panic. Every man thought of his own safety and that of his family and property.' He made for the suburb of Pahagunge, but returned, unmolested, to the city at midday to find the shops shut, the released convicts roaming the streets and the Europeans' houses being looted.

Le Bas, the judge, had gone to his court very early, at about 6.20 a.m. At 9 o'clock he was told that the mutineers from Meerut had occupied the palace and fort and he went to the Main Guard near the Kashmir Gate on the northern wall of the city. Here he found crowds that were less mutinous than curious. But at about 11 o'clock all this changed.

Brigadier Graves commanded the garrison in cantonments on the reverse slopes of the ridge, a little over two miles from the walls of Delhi. Here were the 38th, a detachment of whom were already at the Main Guard under Captain Wallace, the 54th and 74th, all Native Infantry, and some guns under Captain de Tessier. The Brigadier, not realizing that the area of the palace had already fallen to the mutineers and confidently expecting that a relief expedition would come from Meerut within hours, ordered most of the 54th under their colonel, Ripley, to enter the city by the Kashmir Gate; the Infantry were to be accompanied by a field battery of the

Native Artillery under Captain de Tessier.

When the detachment arrived the guard, provided by the 38th, appeared loyal and presented arms to Colonel Ripley. But a body of the 3rd Cavalry, the original Meerut mutineers who had been some three hours in the city, pledged themselves to the King and begun the work of looting and killing, arrived from the palace and barred Ripley's way. Colonel Ripley ordered his detachment to load, but not a sepoy obeyed the order. Then the sowars from Meerut opened fire on the officers. The men of the 54th wavered, broke ranks and joined the mutineers. Ripley fell from his horse and was stabbed to death by the bayonets of his own regiment. By now de Tessier's guns were coming through the gate, and at the sight of the artillery the mutineers of the 38th and 54th fled towards the palace.

The judge, Le Bas, was close to the Main Guard. He could hear the sound of shots and shouts and could smell the powder. As he pressed forward his old and faithful servant caught him by the sleeve and besought him, 'If you want to stay alive you must get out of this place.'

Meanwhile, the ranks of the mutineers were being reinforced at the palace. The Cavalry had arrived from Meerut in the early morning; many of the mutinous infantry, after a night's march, were pouring into the fortress at the east of the city by midday. They were tired and hot as they clattered across the bridge of boats under the burning sun, and when they arrived in the courtyards of the palace showed little respect for the King: bedding was unrolled and cooking pots dumped in the audience hall, the descendant of the Mogul emperors Timur and Akbar was greeted as 'you old man', and one sepoy, with jovial affection, clutched him by the beard. Slightly bemused, after the longest half-day he had ever spent, the 82-year-old poet found himself at last an emperor in his own capital; earlier in the day he had tried to save the lives of Douglas and Fraser – now he was being boisterously hailed as the leader in a holy war against the infidels.

By 1 o'clock the city had fallen; and an officer who was to be present throughout the siege thought it 'beyond doubt, that had even a few squadrons of the Carabineers dashed into the city an hour or two after the mutineers, or had four hundred of the Rifles filed over the bridge about noon', the city would have been saved. Even the King could hardly believe there was no pursuit from Meerut, and he sent a man on a camel to reconnoitre, who was able to report that there were no Europeans for twenty miles to the east. So the slaughter and pillage were to continue.

It was not only the sepoys, but the badmashes, unruly characters from Delhi and the surrounding villages, who made up the marauding bands; to these were added the felons who had been released from the gaol. Such a band trapped the manager, Beresford, on the roof of the Delhi Bank and hacked him to pieces. A mob broke into the offices of the *Delhi Gazette* as the compositors were putting together an issue with news of the disasters of the earlier part of the day. The compositors were killed at their task. A body of rioters broke into the Anglican church of St. James in the northern quarter of the city, ripped up the pews, tore down the memorial plaques, climbed the belfry, gave the bell a peal in derision, and then cut the ropes so that it smashed to pieces on the ground beneath.

One place still held out, and this was the magazine, with Willoughby, Forrest, a handful of European non-commissioned officers and some unreliable lascars. The great gates had been barricaded, and the defenders prepared for a siege. Several times, from noon onwards, messengers came from the King demanding the surrender of the magazine, and then some time after 3 o'clock, the mutineers brought scaling-ladders to the high walls.

The scaling-ladders were not, however, used by the mutineers to enter the arsenal, but by the lascars to make their escape from it. And once they had escaped and abandoned the magazine to the nine Europeans the mutineers from the roofs of the buildings nearby poured fire into the arsenal. The defence was fierce. One of the warrant officers, Buckley, was shot in the arm and Willoughby in the hand. Only when ammunition for musket and cannon was giving out did Willoughby give the order to blow up the magazine. Various powder trails had already been laid, and Conductor Scully came forward to volunteer for the hazardous task of setting fire to them. Neither Willoughby nor Forrest thought for one moment that any inside the magazine would survive the explosion, but so great a prize in arms and ammunition should not fall to the mutineers. With a noise that was heard in Meerut forty miles away, at 4 o'clock in the afternoon of this day of blood, the great arsenal was blown. The encircling walls were flattened, and hundreds of mutineers buried alive. But charred, blackened, their clothing in shreds, Willoughby and Forrest survived to join, by nightfall, the remnants of the European community in Delhi on the ridge to the north of the Kashmir Gate.

The watchers on the ridge saw it all. At first there was 'a puff of white smoke', Le Bas wrote, and then 'a magnificent coronal of red dust rose above the walls.' Seconds later, for the point at which he was standing on the ridge was over two miles from the centre of Delhi, came the great roar of the explosion and the crash of falling masonry.

The third subaltern in the magazine, Raynor, as well as Buckley, Sergeant Stewart and Conductor Shaw survived the explosion and lived to be awarded the Victoria Cross. Scully was killed either by falling masonry or by a sowar, a native cavalry trooper, while trying to escape. Willoughby, though he eventually reached the ridge, was later killed on his way to Meerut.

News of the blowing of the magazine stirred imaginations throughout the empire as no other deed on that day, but the mutineers were not to lack ammunition when the long siege began. Another arsenal had been built to the north of the city, and before dark this was in their hands.

Many escaped. After the killing of Colonel Ripley at the Kashmir Gate Le Bas, seeing now the wisdom of his servant's advice, managed to drop into the ditch that lay the other side of the wall and to scramble, with bullets hissing about his ears, up a steep escarpment and gain the temporary shelter of some scrub. He had even contrived to bring with him some bread, cold meat and a few bottles of beer. Others were with him. There was young Lieutenant Vibart of the 54th and an obese lady, Mrs Forster, who was pushed, screaming, into the ditch. The ground between the water and the northernmost part of the ridge had plenty of cover. The little group hid in the scrub until dusk as there were skirmishers from the mutinous regiments about, and then they made a dash for the ridge. Mrs Forster found it all hard going: at first she was carried and then, her chances of survival slender even if she were to make the ridge, she was abandoned to die in the bushes.

Throughout the afternoon others, men, women and children, had managed to escape the slaughter in the city and had gathered at the Flagstaff Tower at the northern end of the ridge. The tower had been built originally as an observation post, and stood about 150 feet high; it had a parapet at the top, approached by a narrow winding staircase. In the tower itself there were a few small rooms, and here, cramped, dirty, hungry and frightened were huddled the remnants of the European population of Delhi. A civil servant, Wagentreiber, described it all:

'We found a large number of ladies and children collected in a round room some 18 feet in diameter. Servants, male and female, were huddled together with them; many ladies were in a fainting condition from extreme heat and nervous excitement, and all wore that expression of anxiety so near to despair.

'Here were widows mourning their husbands who were murdered, sisters weeping over the report of a brother's death, and some there were whose husbands were still on duty in the midst of disaffected sepoys of whose fate they were as yet ignorant. It was a Black Hole in miniature . . . and I was glad even to stand in the sun to catch a breath of fresh air . . .'

In the late afternoon a bullock cart rumbled up the slope to the Flagstaff Tower. It was piled with the bodies of the officers killed at noon at the Kashmir Gate, and was to remain there, unloaded, until the ridge was retaken on 8 June.

With the dusk came no sign of a relieving party from Meerut. The remaining sepoys on the ridge could not be trusted: there had been consternation among them at the blowing up of the magazine, but some could not conceal their satisfaction at the sight of the bodies in the cart. Le Bas had thought that the 38th had appeared loyal – this, perhaps, out of a personal regard for Brigadier Graves – but even these for the most part had joined the mutineers inside the walls. With dusk came despondency.

'Officers, ladies, children,' wrote Le Bas, 'ayahs and other servants were crowded in and about the Tower. Carriages and buggies were standing close by. The heat was very great. Most of the children were crying . . . Here an officer was haranguing the Sepoys . . . There an anxious group was gathered round the Brigadier . . . Occasionally an officer would gallop off to the Kashmir Gate, carrying some order to Major Abbott . . .'

By the night of 11 May the fortress, the city, the new arsenal, even the ridge itself, had fallen to an enemy so quickly that it was to bemuse and bewilder an empire.

Delhi was now garrisoned wholly by mutinous native troops. There were the original regiments from Meerut. There were those who had come over to the king from the cantonment behind the ridge, men of the 38th, 54th and 74th. As well as this the magazine outside the walls was in their hands and here was a large store of armaments. There were 8,000 muskets, nearly a million cartridges, and two siege-trains. And the reinforcements in men kept coming. The mutineers had open communications to the east, controlled the bridge of boats and the road to Meerut, and, with the ridge abandoned, were able to take up strategic positions in the surrounding villages, at Alipur to the north and Ghazi-ud-din-Nagar to the west.

By Monday the 12th the King had five infantry regiments,

in all about two thousand sepoys, one regiment of 350 cavalry and 180 gunners to man the nine emplacements on the walls. For fifty years, ever since its capture by General Lake in 1803, British engineers had striven to make Delhi impregnable, and their work had been well done.

During the afternoon and evening of the 11th, and on the morning of the 12th, the murdering of Christians and the looting of their houses was orgiastic; there was a feeling among sepoys and badmashes that time was against them, that a European army would descend on them from Meerut and that the work should be done while there was still the chance. But as the Tuesday wore on and there was no sign of avengers the garrison settled to the tasks of defence and organization. At first the commander-in-chief was one of the King's sons; he was later to be replaced by an able subadar of artillery, Mohammed Bakht Khan, who had arrived with the mutinous brigade from Bareilly.

A routine of sorts was established. The sepoys insisted that the King held a durbar every day; sometimes, bewildered by it all and usually tired, the gerontocrat was paraded through the streets of his capital.

'From house to house,' wrote the interpreter Jeewan Lall, 'the unwilling king was distracted by cries and petitions – now from the servants of Europeans who had been murdered, now from the shopkeepers whose shops had been plundered, now from the higher classes whose houses had been broken into – all looked to the king for immediate redress.'

The old man had been borne along by the flood of events. In the morning of the 11th, he had seemed horrified at the entry of the sepoys through the Rajghat Gate, had pleaded with them to disperse, had clutched Fraser and Douglas by the sleeve and told them to escape while they still could. Later in the morning he had ordered a search for their bodies so that they should be given Christian burial. Now, processing in a howdah through the streets of Delhi, he was like a cork on the swelling waves of mutiny.

He was powerless to prevent the massacre of the Christians. To the south of the Chandni Chouk lay the Darao-Ganj quarter where the Eurasians and Indian Christians lived, the clerks and petty officials. Some had been rounded up on the 11th and some murdered on the spot; others had barricaded themselves in their houses or tried to flee to the river; all eventually had been captured and placed in a dungeon, another Black Hole, below the palace. Here they remained for five days. On the 16th they were taken out and told that they were to be removed to another prison. A rope was thrown round the little crowd, mostly of women, to prevent their escape, and they were taken to a courtyard of the palace.

Most of the killing was done by the sword – this because the original firing party had been carelessly positioned, and a sepoy was shot in the first volley. One woman, Mrs Aldwell, pleaded that she was a Moslem and was spared. The corpses of the rest were flung into the Jumna. For the first time since the days of Babur, there was not a Christian soul within the walls of Delhi.

The Governor-General, Lord Canning, was at the capital of the Raj, Calcutta, nine hundred miles away from the horrors of Delhi and Meerut. He had been in India for little more than a year, and his reputation before he succeeded Dalhousie was that of a painstaking, judicious administrator. He had presided so efficiently over the affairs of his department when Postmaster-General under Palmerston that he had been promoted to the cabinet. He had no experience of India; as a younger man Lord Ellenborough had offered him the post of private secretary when he was appointed Governor-General, but Canning had declined. This is how he was to strike *The Times* correspondent, William Howard Russell:

'The Governor-General evinced a remarkable analytical power, an ability of investigation, a habit of appreciating and weighing evidence, a spirit of justice and moderation, and a judicial turn of mind . . . his mode of investigation, abhorrent from all intuitive impulses, and dreading above all things quick decision, is to pursue the forms of the strictest analysis, to pick up every thorn on the path, to weigh it, to consider it and then to cast it aside, or to pile it up with its fellows . . .'

This fair, scrupulous, industrious administrator, of whom the historian Rice Holmes wrote that 'when he should have struck the guilty, he wasted precious moments in taking elaborate precautions against striking the innocent', seems, before his departure for India, to have had a presentiment of disaster. At a banquet he had urged his audience not to forget that though 'the sky of India' was 'serene', 'a small cloud [might] arise, at first no bigger than a man's hand but which, growing larger and larger, [might] at last threaten to burst and overwhelm us with ruin.'

But perception, moderation, and a judicious and meticulous attitude to government were not, in the sweltering May of 1857, what were required of a Governor-General. The 'dread of quick decisions', a virtue in a judge or a scholar, was a vice in a commander. He received a telegram from Agra on the 12th telling him of the rising of the 3rd Cavalry at Meerut and the sacking of the town. Two days later he had details of the fall of Delhi, the abandonment of the ridge and the retreat of the remnants of the garrison and civilians to Kurnal and Amballa. The Governor-General waited eight days before he ordered the mobilization of a European infantry battalion which was in quarters, disengaged, at Barrackpore near Calcutta. He declined the offer of Lord Elphinstone, Governor of Bombay, to send a fast steamer with despatches to England. He waited two days before ordering a British regiment and a regiment of Native Fusiliers in Madras to stand by for embarkation. He waited four days before he sent a steamer to fetch the 35th from Pegu in Burma, five days before asking for reinforcements from the government of Ceylon. He issued, too late, a proclamation intended to reassure the sepoys that the government had no intention of interfering with caste or religion: this only produced the retort from the King of Delhi that 'if the infidels now become mild, it is merely an expedient to save their lives.'

The Commander-in-Chief of the Bengal Army was General the Hon. George Anson, at nearly sixty comparatively young in the gerontocracy that commanded the armies in India. Anson had served as an ensign at Waterloo, but during his subsequent forty-three years of service he had seen no action. London society was surprised when in 1853 he left the racecourses and whist-tables where he was so happy and accepted the appointment of General Officer commanding the Meerut division. Two years later he succeeded as Commander-in-Chief. In March Anson and the whole of the Headquarters staff had moved, in leisurely stages inspecting units on the way, to Simla to spend the hot months in the hills. The nearest telegraph office to this agreeable summer capital was fifty miles away, at the garrison town of Amballa.

Here Major-General Sir Harry Barnard commanded the Sirhind Division. He had recently come to India from the Crimea, where he had succeeded General Simpson as Adjutant-General, that is chief-of-staff, of the British Army. He had with him his son as aide-de-camp, and it was General Barnard's habit to send him daily to the telegraph office to collect messages. On the morning of Wednesday 13 May young Captain Barnard gave his father the last message to come out of Delhi, tapped out by the signaller Brendish before the city fell and he made his way to join the others in the Flagstaff Tower. General Barnard at once sent his son to warn the Commander-in-Chief in Simla, and ordered him, on his own initiative, to warn the 75th at Kasauli to stand by for a march on Delhi.

On arrival Captain Barnard found that Anson was giving a dinner party for two dozen guests whom he did not wish to weary with army matters. He took the despatches and put them under his plate until his guests had gone. It was hours later that he ripped open the envelopes and learnt that his largest garrison had disintegrated and the ancient capital fallen.

On the 15th Anson moved to the garrison at Amballa. Here there were messages waiting for him from John Lawrence, ablest, wisest and most experienced of all the Company's civilian administrators, which urged immediate and swift action. But what was General Anson to do? He had a handful of European troops, the Sikhs in the Punjab appeared loyal, he could count (though perhaps at the time he did not realize it) on the support of the Cis-Sutlej chiefs, but he lacked guns, and the great arsenals were situated far away on the frontiers of the empire. Well might Lawrence write bitingly to the Commander-in-Chief:

'Pray reflect on the whole history of India. Where have we failed when we acted vigorously? Where have we succeeded when guided by timid counsels? Clive with twelve hundred men fought at Plassey, in opposition to the advice of his leading officers, beat forty thousand men and conquered Bengal . . .'

All this was most unfair. There were no points of comparison. Clive, with more than twelve hundred, was faced by a rabble of less than forty thousand. The forces that were to confront Anson were trained, disciplined, well armed; they had secured the city of the greatest strategic importance in all India; they looked as if they were already in control of the Gangetic plain; they had the support of the countryside around Delhi, and the fever of a holy war was in their blood.

To move regiments in the hot weather in India was a cumbersome and slow business. Though the process of building the railways had begun, there were in all India only a few hundred miles of track, and no railway connexion between the garrisons in the north and Delhi or Meerut. The troops marched in darkness to avoid the heat, and they did not travel light. A regiment of five or six hundred would be accompanied by a minimum of a thousand followers – servants, water-carriers, contractors, coolies and men to drive the ox-waggons. Each officer required at the least two camels for his own baggage. These beasts, and the oxen and carts, were hired: when the short contracts ran out, others had to be bargained for. The 'train', as it was called, of a regiment on the march could stretch for over a mile, with scouts leading and skirmishers protecting the flanks. At daybreak the regiment would pitch camp, covering acres of ground with tents, the oxen would roam and graze and wallow in the muddy water, the men would clean weapons, cook and sleep, the camp-followers argue, haggle and sometimes desert; and the whole camp would be encircled by an elaborate system of pickets. Distances were reckoned in 'marches', the ground that could be covered by an infantry regiment in one night. The distance from the garrison at Kurnal to Delhi was about five marches.

Anson put together a small force at Amballa consisting of the 75th Queen's regiment and two regiments of the Bengal Fusiliers, and was annoyed to discover that both regiments were ill-equipped, with only twenty rounds of ammunition per man. Furthermore the force was to march with only three or four days' rations, and was to be prepared to live off the country when this gave out. Before the march Anson decided to try to make contact with General Hewitt at Meerut, but the road to Meerut was believed to be in the control of the mutineers.

Anson had already appointed one of the most controversial characters in the Company's army to his staff. This was Major William Stephen Raikes Hodson, in his mid-thirties, tall, blond and fearless. Hodson had been at Rugby with Thomas Hughes under Doctor Arnold, then spent a short time at Cambridge before joining the Company's service as a subaltern in the infantry. There were in his character elements of the hero, the bully and the confidence trickster. Of all irregular soldiers the most irregular, he had raised a regiment of Guides on the frontier and constructed his own permanent fortifications, picking up the skills of an engineer as he went along. He had been much admired by John Lawrence, commissioner in the Punjab, but his career had been chequered. Hodson had a rough-and-ready method of administration, confusing regimental accounts with his own. Once when a subordinate officer returned to the regiment and asked for his pay, he was told that Hodson had already spent it.

All this led to a long and complicated correspondence and in the end a court-martial, at which Hodson was acquitted, but not before he had been removed from the command of the Guides, and become once again a subaltern – at a time when he had just married, and was already in debt to his father. He was suffering, too, from a sense of grievance: though acquitted by the court-martial, details of the acquittal had been filed away for over a year, and the Headquarters of the Bengal army had not been informed of it.

Hodson volunteered to ride to Meerut from Amballa with despatches, a distance of over a hundred and fifty miles, and he set off with a small escort of Jhind horsemen. It was unnecessary for Hodson to boast that he 'fought his way' to Meerut – that was clearly an exaggeration: to accomplish the mission in seventy-two hours was feat enough. 'Hodson's gallant deeds,' wrote an officer to his wife, 'more resemble a chapter from the life of Bayard or Amadis de Gaul than the doings of a subaltern of the nineteenth century. The only feeling mixed with my admiration for him is envy.' As a result of the information from Hewitt at Meerut, Anson made his plans. He was going to assemble a force at Kurnal, reach Bagpat on 5 June and wait there for a force from Meerut to join him, and then by way of Alipur to march on Delhi and occupy the ridge. But within days the Commander-in-Chief was dead. On 24 May General Barnard – 'a fine gentlemanly old man, but hardly up to his work', was Hodson's opinion of him – arrived at his Headquarters in Kurnal and found Anson in the last stages of cholera. On the 27th he died, handing the command of the expedition to Barnard. 'Barnard, I leave you commanding,' the general told him. 'You know how anxious I was to do my duty. I cannot recover. May success attend you. God bless you. Good-bye.'

No sooner was the Commander-in-Chief buried than the march to Delhi began. The nights were hot, and a halt of five minutes in each hour was ordered. But the morale of the men was high, and the leading companies started songs that were taken up by the men following. 'Along the road came the heavy roll of the guns,' wrote an officer years afterwards, 'mixed with the jangling of bits and the clanking of steel scabbards of the cavalry: the infantry marched behind with a deep, dull tread; camels and bullock-carts, with innumerable sutlers and camp servants, toiled along for miles in the rear; while gigantic elephants stalked over bush and stone by the side of the road . . .'

The march was a splendid achievement. By 5 June the expedition was at Alipur, only twelve miles from the Delhi walls and awaiting the arrival of the force from Meerut. Barnard's achievement did much to dispel the mounting criticism – not always deserved – of the dilatoriness of Anson, to reassure those in Calcutta that something, at last, was being done.

Other things had been done, too, on that six days' march beside battling with the heat, and the dust and sand that was sometimes ankle-deep. During the day villages that lay in the path of the expedition were searched, courts-martial hastily set up and the hangings of those suspected of crimes against the 'feringi' (Europeans) began. At one village five men were seized for having grossly insulted two ladies escaping on foot from Delhi. They were convicted, although some of the witnesses against them had disappeared, and were sentenced to be hanged. For the news of the massacre of the Christians on 16 May had reached the British soldiery and, wrote Rice Holmes:

'Officers, as they went to sit on courts-martial, swore that they would hang the prisoners, guilty or innocent; and, if anyone dared to lift up his voice against such indiscriminate vengeance, he was instantly silenced by the clamour of his angry comrades. Prisoners, condemned to death after a hasty trial, were mocked and tortured by ignorant privates before their execution, while educated officers looked on and approved.' The demand for vengeance swelled slowly, vengeance for Colonel Ripley, for Miss Clifford, for the fifty murdered Christians in the palace courtyard. The demand was to grow until it ended in an orgy of slaughter three months later inside the walls of the Mogul City.

Chapter Three

MESSIAH

'We are told in the Bible that stripes shall be meted out according to faults . . .'

By the time that Anson – belatedly or not – had made his plans for the march on Delhi, all was anarchy at Meerut and in the countryside that surrounded it. The 'Goojurs', hereditary robbers, plundered and murdered now that the army had disintegrated. Old disputes over boundaries were revived, and quarrels that had long smouldered were settled with matchlock and spear. Still General Hewitt delayed, and at first seems to have made little effort to restore order. He did, however, proclaim martial law, but there was no one with the energy to enforce it. He had no light cavalry to send to the rebellious villages – even though a lieutenant in the mounted police had offered to collect thirty-six volunteers, an offer coldly declined by the general. It was not until a fortnight after the original revolt of the 3rd Cavalry that Hewitt sent a small force of dragoons to try to restore order in the villages. Rice Holmes wrote that, until the few dragoons 'emerged from their seclusion, the natives believed that not a single Englishman remained alive in Meerut.' In fact there were more than a thousand, including a battalion of the 60th Rifles, 'there was only wanting a general to command them.'

Nevertheless, General Hewitt thought that he could best serve by remaining in the garrison, and so the force from Meerut that was to meet Barnard's outside Delhi was to be commanded by Brigadier Archdale Wilson. Wilson had shared Hewitt's unenviable reputation for inactivity when mutiny broke out at Meerut: he had shown the same blindness to the signs of growing discontent, the same reluctance to pursue the mutineers, the same desire to remain in a garrison no longer worth defending. But he, unlike General Hewitt, was to redeem his reputation by early June. This elderly brigadier with twinkling eyes and an imperial beard had qualities of a sort which his superior lacked: 'he is a gentlemanly, quiet, steady old fellow,' wrote Colonel Keith Young, 'looks to everything himself and gives clear and distinct orders', and he had the capacity of making those under him 'feel much at their ease'. The column that left Meerut on 27 May, ominously the day that Anson died of cholera at Kurnal, was composed of two squadrons of Carabineers, a detachment of the 60th Rifles ('a fine regiment, so totally different to every other', wrote Major Reid of the Gurkhas), one light field battery of artillery, some horse artillery under Major Tombs, and a body of Indian sappers and irregulars. Spirits were high and there was a general desire to avenge the slaughter in Delhi. Hervey Greathed, the commissioner at Meerut, who was accompanying the force noted that 'a number of men of the Rifles whistled marches and popular airs, as we went along, very well; and all are cheery.'

By 30 May the column had reached the village of Ghazi-ud-din-Nagar, a few miles to the east of Delhi, and here they met resistance from the mutineers for the first time. In front of the village ran the river Hindun, a tributary of the Jumna, spanned by a suspension bridge. A strong force from Delhi was posted on high ground on the western bank of the river. At about 4 o'clock in the afternoon fire from the heavy guns of the mutineers' artillery checked the advance of Wilson's column.

There followed a short and decisive battle. Wilson sent a company of the 60th Rifles to hold the suspension bridge. Meanwhile the horse artillery were sent northwards along the bank of the river which they crossed – in spite of the high banks and quicksands in the river's bed – and attacked and turned the enemy's left flank, Tombs' artillery silencing the guns on the rising ground. Then the 60th and Carabineers moved in on the main body of the mutineers, who fled, routed, towards Delhi.

The defeated force was not well received on its return to the city where there were taunts and jeers for the first of the victorious captors of Delhi to lose a battle against the feringi. With reinforcements, they returned to the Hindun next morning, Whit Sunday. They found an advanced picket of Wilson's force in front of the suspension bridge and opened fire on it with artillery from about a mile away. The rifles again secured the suspension bridge and Tombs returned the enemy fire with his horse artillery. Wilson ordered a general advance, and for the second time in twenty-four hours the mutineers retreated in a rout. But Wilson's forces were prevented, wrote Hervey Greathed, from pursuing their enemy and preventing them from carrying away their guns: they were parched with thirst and many fainted under the burning sun of the hottest time of year. Wilson had acted with a decisiveness that he had not shown three weeks earlier in Meerut. The first engagement had been won with small loss. But this victory, unfairly, was later played down by General Nicholson: 'By all accounts,' he wrote to John Lawrence, 'he (Wilson) was driven into fighting at the Hindun, and could not help himself.'

The force from Meerut remained encamped at Ghazi-ud-din-Nagar for four more days, when they were ordered to join the column under Barnard at Alipur to the west of the city, which Wilson reached on 7 June. There had also arrived at Alipur a siege-train put together at the garrison town of Phillaur in the north. An officer, George Campbell, saw it pass through Kurnal a few days before, and it did not impress him: 'It looked a very trumpery affair,' he wrote, 'with which to bombard and take a great fortified city.'

Hodson was held in the greatest esteem by General Barnard. On the 6th he was summoned to the Headquarters tent where there was a council of war in progress. 'I have always trusted to Hodson's intelligence,' Barnard told the council, 'and have the greatest confidence in his judgment. I will be guided by what he can tell me now.' So Barnard's first action on occupying Alipur was to send Hodson on reconnaissance to discover the disposition of the enemy forces outside Delhi. At night, with a small body of Indian cavalry, Hodson reached the walls and returned at dawn the next day to report. He told Barnard that 'about two thousand of the rebels [had] come out of Delhi, and put themselves in position to bar our road.' The enemy held a strong position about five miles north-west of the city and on the direct route from Alipur. This was at the little walled village of Badli-ke-Serai, protected on one flank by an impassable water-course, on the other by the Najafgarh Jheel canal. This position was defended in the front by a battery of artillery, by canal and water-course on the flanks. The whole position commanded the Grand Trunk Road.

Barnard decided on an attack at daybreak on 8 June. A flank attack was impossible, so the village was to be attacked simultaneously from the front and the rear. Infantry and light and heavy artillery were to advance down the Grand Trunk Road, while Colonel Hope Grant with cavalry and two troops of horse artillery was to cross the canal south of the enemy's position and to attack the left rear.

After the gruelling night marches, with the beginning of an epidemic of cholera, and with the oppressive heat, many of Barnard's force were in the field hospital. But on that night of tension before the battle for Badli-ke-Serai many of them, wrote the chaplain Cave-Browne, 'rose painfully from their beds, and swore that they would remain in hospital no longer.' As the news that an attack was to be made at dawn passed from soldier to soldier spirits rose and some 'were almost consumed by the rising fire of their passion.'

Before day broke the force that was to attack the village from the north-west advanced along the Grand Trunk Road – two infantry brigades under Brigadier Graves and Colonel Showers – while Hope Grant and the cavalry and field artillery had begun their long flanking movement to reach the rear of the enemy position. But the two infantry brigades were not able to move at the same speed. Colonel Showers was only a short distance from the walls of the serai, (fortified village), when he discovered that the brigade under Graves had been held up two miles in his rear by some baggage carts that had been allowed to block the road. It was then that the enemy opened a savage fire on the advanced, and unsupported, brigade. Barnard ordered the 75th Queen's regiment and the Bengal Fusiliers to charge the batteries. There was fierce fighting with no quarter asked or given. Soon the rebels lost ground and began to retreat towards Delhi, when Hope Grant, who had by then reached the rear of the enemy position, hurled in the 9th Lancers and ordered a flanking fire from the horse artillery. With the capture of the batteries in front of their position the mutineers had begun an orderly retreat; it now became a rout. 'Here we are, safe and sound,' scribbled Hodson to his wife in pencil using the top of a drum as a desk, 'after having driven the enemy out of their position in the cantonments up to and into the walls of Delhi.'

The strategic importance of the victory was immense. Barnard now controlled the Grand Trunk Road and was secure in his communications to the north and west. But all this had been at the cost of heavy casualties in a force already wasted by disease and exhaustion. The way to the ridge was now open: with the victory at Badli-ke-Serai the siege of Delhi really began.

While the relief expeditions from Meerut, Amballa and Kurnal were converging on Delhi, there was activity in the newly-occupied lands of the Punjab and on the Afghan frontier that was to change the course of the mutiny, preserve an empire and avenge the murdered Christians. Here the dour and capable John Lawrence was the Chief Commissioner. It was he who had urged action as soon as he had news of the fall of Delhi and who had written so scathingly to Anson at Amballa.

On the frontier the tasks facing soldier and civilian administrator were different from those in the older, more settled provinces of the Raj. The lands of the Punjab had been conquered in the 'forties and even Peshawar itself, the great frontier garrison, had recently been part of Afghanistan. There were fierce tribes in the hills; there was the fear of a Russian presence in Afghanistan poised to begin the erosion of the empire. Here in the north-west the administrators had worked with an almost missionary zeal. 'When I think of all that has been done,' wrote one of them, 'when I recall the state of the country before the annexation, and the marvellous change that came over it in the course of so few years, I cannot but regret, that such men are not found for the other dark places of this globe.' The achievement had been impressive: in a few years feudal troops had been disbanded and a police force established in their place, roads had been built, protection given to life and property, the foundations laid for a system of education and civil justice; there was freedom of religion, freedom of trade and freedom of movement.

All this had been done, for the most part, by men of stern religious faith, men like Herbert Edwardes, the Civil Commissioner at Peshawar – an able, uncomplicated, jovial, self-confident muscular Christian, one who could punish the guilty with severity, and then discuss the meaning of a passage of Holy Writ. His faith was in the truths of the Bible and in the blessings of Western civilization – justice, the rule of law, even 'the principle of utility'. These were what should bring light to 'the dark places of this globe'.

Under him at Peshawar was a man of a different stamp. He was John Nicholson who, at the age of thirty-five, was already a lieutenant-colonel and was soon to be a brigadier. He was a man of brooding good looks, with large dark eyes whose pupils, we are told by a subaltern who served under him, dilated at times of excitement, a pallid complexion, a long straight nose, a black spade beard. 'He was a man cast in a giant mould, with massive chest and powerful limbs, and an expression ardent and commanding, with a dash of roughness . . . There was something of immense strength, talent, and resolution in his whole gait and manner, and a power of ruling men on high occasion . . .' Nicholson's character is one that reappears, like a leitmotive, through the annals of military history: there was something of him in Lawrence of Arabia and possibly in Orde Wingate. He possessed abundant courage, but it was not a courage that came from self-assurance: in him there was a spirit of lonely self-questioning, of tortured complexity and contradiction. Dispensing with courts-martial, he would hang mutineers by the score on the spot – and then retire to his tent to weep.

By the time the news of the fall of Delhi had reached Peshawar Nicholson was already a legend on the north-west frontier. A group of fakirs believed that he was a reincarnation of Brahma and founded a sect for the worship of 'Nikkul Seyn'. These votaries used to be beaten by their god, which they took as a sign of his deity: 'he is a just god, and punishes us for our good.' In this dark, lonely, brooding spirit sadism struggled with sentiment. He had no women friends or correspondents apart from his mother in Dublin; and the affection he had for a few men friends – his younger brother, his Pathan servant, Herbert Edwardes – was rock-like in its constancy.

'If ever there is a desperate deed to be done in India,' wrote Herbert Edwardes to the Governor-General in early 1857, 'John Nicholson is the man to do it.' He had already achieved much in a short time. With a disdain for the conventions and an arrogant and lonely indifference to the opinion of others, he had 'reduced the most ignorant and bloodthirsty people in the Punjab to such a state of order and respect for law that in the last year of his charge there was no crime of murder or highway robbery committed or even attempted.'

It was not only due to Nicholson, but to other soldiers and civilians also – Herbert Edwardes, Robert Montgomery, Brigadier Sydney Cotton – that all the ferocity of the mutineers at Meerut, Delhi, Lucknow and Cawnpore did not spread to the Punjab. They acted with speed and decisiveness, in contrast to the hesitancy born of a misplaced trust that had been shown by Hewitt and Wilson. At signs of disaffection a regiment was disarmed; the mutinous were promptly hanged or 'blown away'. Justice was rough, but sure. As early as 12 May the Judicial Commissioner Robert Montgomery learnt of the events at Meerut. He called a conference of civilians, military and police which decided to disarm the four native infantry regiments whom Montgomery, on good authority, believed to be waiting for a favourable opportunity to throw aside their allegiance. A general parade was ordered for 13 May.

The disarming was to take place at the garrison at Mian-Mir. Only a few officers of the garrison knew the purpose of the parade, and a ball which had been arranged for the night of the 12th took place – to postpone it would have aroused suspicions – that reminded some of the Duchess of Richmond's ball on the eve of Quatre Bras. In the early morning the garrison paraded, native troops outnumbering Europeans by eight to one, with the four native infantry regiments in the centre, European troops on the right and Indian cavalry on the left. The order disbanding the 34th at Barrackpore was read to the regiments, and the command to ground arms was given. The sepoys hesitated, whereupon they heard the sharp words of command given to the 81st Queen's regiment on the right: 'Eighty-first, load!' and saw the portfires in the hands of the European gunners. The arms of more than two thousand sepoys were grounded in order, in the euphemistic words that were read to the regiments, 'to shield them from the temptation' to mutiny. Immediately after the parade a detachment of the 81st was sent to Lahore where the small native garrison was disarmed and the fort occupied. Simple plans quickly executed saved the Punjab: perhaps they saved the empire itself.

But there were other garrisons in the Punjab, Amritsar, Ferozpur, Multan and the arsenal at Phillaur on the Grand Trunk Road. To the authorities in these places Montgomery sent letters of warning of the danger and the example made of the four regiments at Mian-Mir. At Ferozpur there was a mutiny. Here an order to ground arms was refused and sepoys and badmashes sacked the town before marching to join the rebels in Delhi, but few reached the city, most being dispersed by a pursuing European regiment.

Three weeks before the ridge was retaken, the Punjab had been secured. From here, on the suggestion of Nicholson, was to come a third relieving force, the 'movable column'.

Through the latter half of May, Nicholson was stamping out mutiny in the north-west. He had a strangely ambivalent attitude to India and the Indians: though the inspirer of fanatical personal loyalty and single-minded in the pursuit of a kind of military excellence, he could write to his mother: 'I dislike India and its inhabitants more every day, and would rather go home on £200 a year than live like a prince here.' Admittedly that had been years earlier, after the terrible defeats in Afghanistan, the massacre of a British force, the surrender of European officers to Asiatics. Now he was pursuing rebels with zeal. What need of courts-martial? He could trust his instincts and the evidence of his eyes; and, as he often said, the punishment for mutiny was death. On one occasion officers in a mess-tent were commenting irritably that dinner was half an hour late. Nicholson came in and laconically apoligized to them. 'I am sorry for the delay, gentlemen. I have just hanged the cooks.'

But he could show mercy. At the end of May there was a general mutiny of the 55th Native Infantry. 'I must say a few words,' he wrote to Herbert Edwardes, 'for some of the Fifty-Fifth prisoners . . . I would . . . temper stern justice with mercy, and spare the Sikhs and young recruits. Blow away all the rest, by all means, but spare boys scarcely out of their childhood, and men who were really loyal and respectful up to the moment when they allowed themselves to be carried away in a panic by the mass.'

Many leaders of the mutinous regiments were blown away from the guns. John Lawrence himself suggested that the most guilty should 'be shot or blown away from the guns, as may be most expedient.' Captain Charles Griffiths witnessed a scene

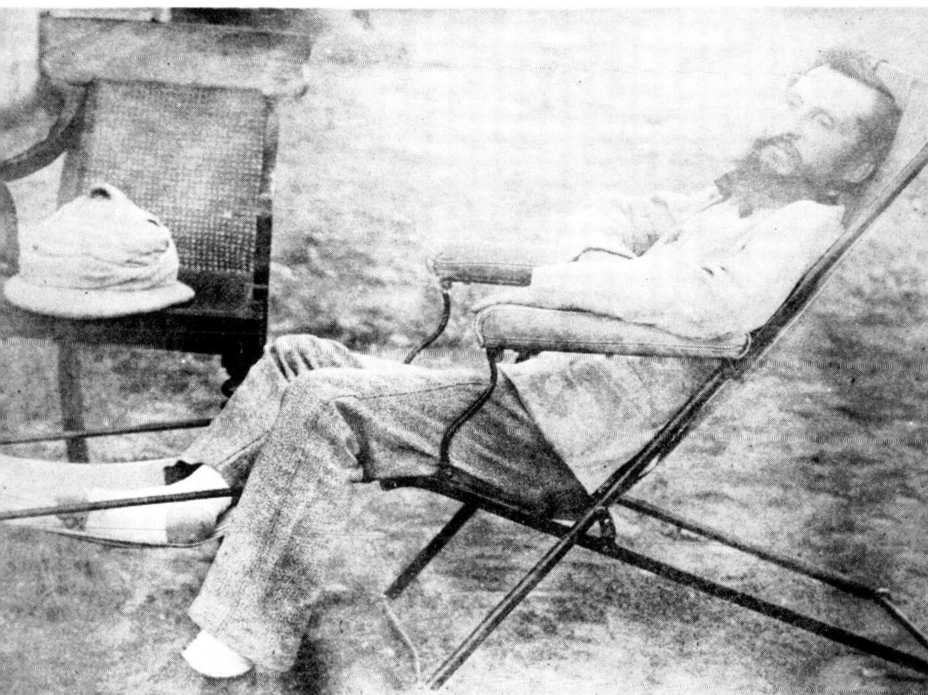

Above Officers in the lines behind the ridge.
Below Captain Alexander Taylor, Bengal Engineers. Nicholson on his death-bed was to say: 'Remember to tell them that Alex Taylor took Delhi.'

Above The Flagstaff Tower on the ridge, where the Europeans took refuge on the night of 11 May.
Below The Magazine in Delhi, blown on the afternoon of 11 May.

of 'blowing away' on a sultry morning in mid-May. There were fourteen condemned – twelve for the guns and two to be hanged. The garrison marched to the execution parade with bands playing. A European battery of six 9-pounder guns had been drawn up and the twelve condemned were formed up in two ranks behind him, their eyes unbandaged. On the word of command the six in the front rank marched a few paces forward so that they were level with the muzzles of the guns, and, showing no signs of emotion, were tied with the small of the back over the mouth of the gun; they even watched with a professional interest the lighting of the portfires. But before the flames were put to the charges the silence was broken, and, wrote Griffiths, 'the condemned poured out maledictions on our heads; and in their language, one most rich in expletives, they exhausted the whole vocabulary.' After the execution the band struck up again and the troops were marched back to their lines.

William Hodson saw ten blown away in Peshawar. 'It was a horrid sight . . . a regular shower of human fragments of heads, of arms, of legs, appeared in the air through the smoke.' But, he reported, there was no feeling of pity. 'So great is the disgust we all feel for the atrocities committed by the rebels' that there was 'perfect callousness . . . depicted on every European's face; a look of grim satisfaction could even be seen in the countenances of the gunners serving the guns.' There was a grisly accompaniment to all this – due to an oversight backing-boards had not been erected and gunners and witnesses were spattered with burning flesh.

But all this was not enough for Nicholson. In May and June he was writing to Herbert Edwardes urging harsher punishments: 'let us propose a bill for the flaying alive, impalement or burning of the murderers of the women and children at Delhi. The idea of simply hanging the perpetrators of such atrocities is maddening . . . We are told in the Bible that stripes shall be meted out according to faults, and if a hanging was sufficient punishment for such wretches, it is too severe for ordinary mutineers. If I had them in my power today, and

I knew that I were to die tomorrow, I would inflict the most excruciating tortures I could think of on them with a perfectly easy conscience.'

On the day following the battle of Badli-ke-Serai, 8 June, General Barnard's Delhi Field Force occupied the ridge, but the lack of soil and the hard rock made the construction of defences a difficult task for the engineers. The ridge was a bare spine of a hill, mostly quartz, about two miles in length. It was protected at the north by the Jumna, at that point unfordable and so wide that artillery on its eastern bank could do little damage to forces on the left of the British position, from which there was a magnificent view of the whole of the city. 'The eye ran along the wide circuit of its ramparts,' wrote one officer, 'with their picturesque gates and bastions half hid among the trees, resting on the palace of the old Mogul conquerors with its green gardens and lofty, red walls . . . It seemed half hidden in green, every hovel having its little enclosure and garden. The giant domes and lofty minarets of the Jumma Masjid towered above all, as if reared by the hands of Titans.'

It was here, and on this day, that Hodson was reunited with his Guides – the irregulars whom he had raised and trained, and then had command of them taken from him. They gave him a rapturous welcome 'cheering and shouting and crowding round me like frantic creatures' he told his wife. 'They seized my bridle, hands and feet, and literally threw themselves down before the horse with the tears streaming down their faces.' Some of the officers thought he was being mobbed, and so he was, 'but for joy, not for mischief.'

The cantonments that had been abandoned on the night of 11 May lay behind the ridge, and these, misguidedly perhaps, were burnt by Barnard when he arrived. The left flank of the British position was protected by the Jumna. On the right, and lying behind the most southerly spurs of the ridge, was the village of Sabsi Mandi, to the south of that the suburb of Kishenganj. The left of Barnard's position at the northernmost point of the ridge was over two miles from the city walls at the Kashmir Gate, the right of his position only a little over half a mile from the Kabul Gate. The whole position that he had taken up covered only a fraction of the Delhi walls; to the south and to the east the defenders had unlimited access; reinforcements and supplies could pour in through the Calcutta Gate and across the bridge of boats.

Along the ridge there were four buildings that provided defensive positions. On the left there was the Flagstaff Tower which had provided a temporary shelter for the fugitives from the city a month before. In the centre there was an empty mosque and an observatory. On the right, almost at the end of the ridge, there was the large empty mansion of a Mahratta chief, known as Hindu Rao's house; it was spacious, with out-buildings and a small garden laboriously made from earth carried up to the ridge. Barnard posted pickets at all these points of vantage. The ground between the ridge and the city was covered in scrub which provided excellent cover, and there were a few small villages. About a mile to the east of the Flagstaff Tower and a mile and a half from the Kashmir Gate stood Metcalfe's house, an imposing mansion with porticoes surrounded by a verandah, in a park of a thousand acres, an English country house, furnished as such, that had been set down on the burning plains of the Indian Empire by the Chief Magistrate's father. To the south of this, little more than half a mile from the Kashmir Gate, was another large house known as Ludlow Castle. It seemed likely that these two positions would be the tactical prizes most keenly contended for.

The city itself was not only protected by the seven miles of wall, forty feet in height, with its ten massive gates and numerous gun emplacements; the walls themselves were also surrounded by a ditch thirty feet wide and thirty-five feet deep, with, in most parts, a rough and dangerous counterscarp. With the artillery that Barnard had in early June it was not possible to breach the walls, and without a breach the city could not be taken by storm.

A group of young and ambitious officers, however, was urging Barnard to assault without delay, among them Wilberforce

Greathed and William Hodson, whose reputation after his ride from Kurnal to Meerut and his daring reconnaissance on the eve of the battle of Badli-ke-Serai was considerable. A council of war was held and it was agreed to attempt a *coup de main* on 13 June: at dawn the artillery should try to blow open the two gates nearest to the ridge, two columns should enter the city, passing along the ramparts to the right and left and capture the gun emplacements. The plan, with the paucity of artillery and men at Barnard's disposal, would have had no chance of success; and because of a misunderstanding it was never even attempted. Brigadier Graves was the field officer of the day, and he was given a verbal order to relieve some European troops from the pickets so that they could join the attacking force, and to replace them by sepoys. Questioning the wisdom of the order and doubting the loyalty of the sepoys he rode to Barnard's tent and persuaded him to countermand the attack, and a certain disaster was avoided.

The Delhi Field Force settled to a long, wearisome period of waiting for reinforcements from the Punjab, for more artillery and for a siege-train. No sudden *coup de main* could take a position so nearly impregnable.

It was the hottest season of the year and the Delhi cantonments, as the chaplain the Reverend James Rotton said, 'had proved to be the most unhealthy station for troops in the north-west provinces.' Conditions in that early June were appalling. There was the heat and the flies. It was 'insupportable,' wrote Charles Griffiths, 'the thermometer under the shade of my tent marking 112 degrees; and to add to our misery there came upon us a plague of flies . . . They literally darkened the sky, descending in myriads and covering everything in our midst . . . and we knew that they owed their existence to, and fattened on, the putrid corpses of dead men and animals which lay rotting and unburied in every direction . . . the air was tainted with corruption . . .' The flies also concerned the surgeon Edward Hare. 'I tried every known poison,' he wrote, 'but in vain.' At last he applied glue and sugar to sheets of paper to hang over the beds in his field hospital; these, black with flies, were taken down by the sweepers each day and destroyed in heaps.

As soon as the ridge was occupied there began the steady bombardment of the guns from the walls, the daily harassing raids across the no-man's-land that lay between the ditches outside Delhi and the foot of the ridge. 'At first,' wrote Rotton, 'it was literally nothing but fighting by day, and watching and expecting to renew the conflict by night.' The troops had little rest when they were in the pickets: those in the camp often slept clothed and under arms. The chaplain made frequent visits to the pickets where he saw 'the same hands everlastingly employed in the same work.'

Until 19 June there were a few women and children in the camp, but on that day General Barnard gave the order that they were to be evacuated to Meerut by elephant. Harriet Tytler, wife of a captain, was eight months pregnant and was allowed to stay. Two days later she gave birth prematurely to a son. The birth was considered a good omen by the British soldiers and was greeted by them as the first of the reinforcements. He was christened by the Reverend James Rotton with the name Stanley Delhi Field Force. The child was born with dysentery; he was not expected to live for more than a week. 'There he lay,' wrote Harriet Tytler, 'near the opening of the van, with only a small piece of flannel thrown over him, the setting sun shining brightly on his little face and nothing but the sound of alarms, calls and shot and shell as lullabies . . .' The covering of the van was not watertight and, wrote Mrs Tytler, 'in a few moments we were drenched, baby and all, to the skin.' Captain Tytler found shelter for them in the Bell of Arms (arms store) and brought fresh straw. There Harriet and 'Delhi Field Force' remained for three months, until the city was captured and they had very different quarters in a palace.

The force on the ridge was growing. The commander of a body of irregulars, Captain Henry Daly of the Guides, had received news of the fall of Delhi on 13 May while his corps was at Mardan in the Punjab. He marched them at once to Rawalpindi and was told to proceed to Delhi. The corps was a large one, six companies of infantry and three troops of cavalry, all recruited from the martial tribes of the frontier, raised and commanded, until his temporary disgrace, by that genius in improvisation, William Hodson. They were not compelled to wear the heavy constricting uniforms of the European soldiers, but 'their own loose, dusty shirts, and sun-proof, sword-proof turbans.' The march was made in incredible time: the Guides averaged twenty-nine miles in a night, and on 9 June arrived behind the ridge 'with a fine swinging stride'. Within three hours they were in action against a party of mutineers from the city.

The Sirmoor battalion of Gurkhas under Major Reid had started from Dehra Dun in mid-May. Their diminutive commanding officer ('a smart officer . . . his men like him') had been at school with Hervey Greathed. On their way to Delhi from the north the Sirmoor battalion had mopped up rebels in the villages that lay in their path. On the 21st they surprised a body of them; eighteen were tried by a drum-head court-martial and shot. A few days later there was a technical hitch while they were hanging some brahmins, and the ropes broke. As soon as the feet of the condemned touched the ground, Major Reid gave the order: 'Two files to the front, quick march, ready, present,' and the Gurkhas fired 'just as if they had been firing at a target on parade'. To the Sirmoor battalion was to fall the hardest task of any on the ridge; they were to hold the bombarded, beleaguered house of Hindu Rao on the right flank.

On 1 July Captain Griffiths arrived with a wing of the 61st Queen's regiment. He was met by a body of the Carabineers four miles from the ridge, and was escorted rapturously into the camp with the bands playing 'Cheer, boys, cheer'. At about this time, too, the young Frederick Roberts – later to be the best loved of all Victorian field-marshals – joined the camp. On his way he passed the corpses of those killed at the battle of Badli-ke-Serai and noted that they had been mummified in the sand; later he was to wish that whatever it was in the atmosphere of Badli which had preserved the bodies from corruption could have done the same for the corpses on the ridge.

At the end of June had arrived the most valuable reinforcements of all – until the arrival of Nicholson and his column – in the persons of two officers. One of them was Brigadier Neville Chamberlain, an officer of the frontier tradition, able, intelligent and resourceful. He in collaboration with Herbert Edwardes and John Nicholson (to whom he had just handed over the command) had raised the movable column in the Punjab, and he was appointed Adjutant-General to the Field Force. The other arrival was one of the most knowledgeable military engineers in the Company's service, the Scotsman Colonel Richard Baird Smith, an authority on irrigation who had spent most of his service with the Madras army. He was peculiarly fitted for his task on the ridge: only the year before he had been engaged in improving the canals that surrounded Delhi. During this time he wrote to a friend that 'almost every day was spent in examining parts of the city', and from this he had acquired 'a tolerably minute knowledge of the important features of the ground both inside and outside the place.' Baird Smith was to provide the technical genius in the planning of the final assault on Delhi.

The enemy meanwhile were making assaults on the British position on the ridge. 23 June was the centenary of the battle of Plassey, a day of omen for both the besiegers and the besieged. Many of the mutineers believed in a prophecy that the rule of the British would last for only one hundred years, and both Hindus and Moslems in the city had been harangued on this theme. At dawn on the 23rd they launched an attack on the village of Sabsi Mandi, the rebellious sepoys wearing their British medals. The objective of the attack was Hindu Rao's house: the mutineers were able to take up positions and to hold them for several hours to the south and rear of the British picket. They were not driven off until the afternoon. The anniversary of Plassey had been, commented Colonel Henry Norman, 'a wretchedly anxious day'.

Inspired by their new commander Bakht Khan the rebels made another assault on 3 July. In the evening Hodson saw their position outside the gates and several miles to the south of the British camp. Before dawn the next morning a contingent composed mostly of newly joined troops anxious to prove themselves against the mutineers was sent to intercept them. There was an exchange of artillery fire: the mutineers withdrew, and the British settled down to breakfast under the shade of some trees by the canal bank, the food being brought out from the camp by white-robed mess servants.

But while the infantry were taking their ease in the shade – Charles Griffiths was sharing a bottle of beer with a friend – the mutineers made a surprise attack. There was a volley from some dense woodland on the flank, and many of the British were killed. Some elephants which had been brought to transport the wounded back to the camp panicked at the noise, and raced along the banks of the canal to disappear into the jungle. The British infantry, their 'stand easy' interrupted, then re-formed to confront the mutineers in a clearing. They were greatly outnumbered and advanced under a heavy musket fire. The day was saved by Major Tombs and the horse artillery who galloped past Griffiths and the infantry, unlimbered their guns, and started to shell the mutineers, who turned and made for the gates of the city.

Casualties among the British had been heavy. Many were killed in the surprise attack on the banks of the canal; many died of sunstroke, their faces turning black. In their retreat the mutineers had left a great deal of their equipment – belts, pouches and footwear. Colonel Young saw the irregular cavalry returning to the camp with their horses piled high with this booty. Henry Daly was elated by the ease with which so large a party of mutineers had been routed: 'Cowardly loons – little honour they do us in fighting. They *never stand* . . .' But Archdale Wilson, now showing that despondency that was to cloud his actions during the coming weeks, was disappointed at it all. The stream of letters he was sending to his wife did not make cheerful reading. 'We have been making another mess of it today, using up four corps where two would have done, and losing the chance to follow up the insurgents' retreat and make something decisive of it. Our position is now worse than ever . . .'

At about this time, too, the enemy were being reinforced. When Chamberlain and Baird Smith arrived on the ridge, mutineers from the Rohilkand poured into Delhi. In early July the mutineers attempted to intercept some British convoys at Alipur but were foiled. This was their one move: if the Delhi garrison had had an able general he would have seen that the vital tactic was to cut the British lines of communication to the north, and this might even have prevented the arrival of Nicholson's column. Baird Smith saw the danger, and in the first days of July he put his engineers to work destroying the bridges over the Western Jumna Canal and the Najafgarh Jheel. He even attempted vainly to destroy the bridge of boats which was the enemy's life-line.

Barnard was cheered by the arrival of Baird Smith, and the general's last contribution to the Delhi Field Force was to give the engineer his head in the matter of defences. But Barnard was by now showing signs of hesitancy and uncertainty, giving no clear lead as he was himself unsure, listening at first to those who advised assault and then countermanding his own orders. Of an action fought at the end of June an engineer officer wrote of the lack of direction from above: 'the great want . . . was the want of a head; officers lead on their parties without any method or arrangement.' Barnard was, however, loved by those who served under him. Rice Holmes described him as 'a perfect gentleman, the courteous open-handed host, the thoughtful, tender friend'; Hodson wrote that he woke one night to find 'the kind old man standing at [my] bedside, carefully covering [me] up from the draught'. Not to officers only did he show compassionate courtesy: he was loved by the private soldiers, and admired, not for his decisions, but for his great industry and constant presence among them. But by the early days of July the anxiety was proving too great a strain, and sleeplessness had debilitated him. Colonel Baird Smith noted 'a certain heaviness and dimness of the eye, not at all natural to him,' when he was summoned to a three-hour interview in the general's tent. During the day of 5 July Barnard suffered the first convulsions of cholera. Before nightfall he was dead.

The new commander of the Delhi Field Force lasted only twelve days. He was Major-General Thomas Reed, a divisional commander from the Punjab. He went through some plans for an assault drawn up for him by Baird Smith, decided that the Force was not strong enough to put them into effect, and, on the 17th, wasted by disease as Anson and Barnard had been before him, he handed over the command of all the forces on the ridge to Brigadier Archdale Wilson and left for the hills.

For a fortnight in mid-June there was a controversy of great importance among those in command on the frontier. John Lawrence was convinced of the supreme, the overriding importance of the capture of Delhi, to achieve which he was prepared to make any sacrifice, even to follow a course that might have led to the abandonment of the Punjab. On 9 June he wrote to Herbert Edwardes suggesting that all the European troops in the Peshawar valley be sent to the relief of Delhi, and that Dost Mohammed of Afghanistan be invited to garrison the valley; if he were to prove a faithful ally Peshawar should be ceded to him in perpetuity. The suggestion was desperate: it was tantamount to saying that either Delhi and the Gangetic plain, or the Punjab, would inevitably be forfeit, and that Delhi should be retained.

The suggestion amazed Nicholson, Edwardes and Cotton. The abandonment of the Punjab would, they knew, be taken by the tribes as a sign of weakness. Moreover, it was of supreme strategic importance for the reconquest of the whole of India. It was vital, they pointed out, to keep an open route to the ports of the north-west, for if all failed at Delhi and on the ridge the Raj might yet be re-established by a sea-borne invasion. Edwardes wrote a strong plea to his chief on the 25th: 'whatever takes place in Central India, we shall stand in a firm and honourable attitude if we maintain the capitals on the sea, and the frontiers here. Between the two it is all a family quarrel, an insurrection in our own house . . . If General Reed, with all the men you have sent him, cannot get into Delhi, let Delhi go.' The matter was referred to the Governor-General. Lawrence had presented Canning with what amounted to an ultimatum, had even suggested the wording of the cables that Canning was to give in reply – either 'Hold on to Peshawar to the last', or 'You may act as may appear expedient regarding Peshawar.' Canning decided in favour of Edwardes. Peshawar was not to be denuded of troops, and the vigorous prosecution of the siege of Delhi was to continue.

Details for the forming of the movable column were drawn up in the Punjab, but the question of command was to be a problem. Sydney Cotton, Herbert Edwardes, John Nicholson and Neville Chamberlain all seemed to have a claim and all were eager to lead the new force. It was General Reed who referred the matter to the commander-in-chief; the answer came by cable, that it was to be Chamberlain, until he was required on the ridge to head the staff of the Delhi Field Force.

The atmosphere of these conferences at Rawalpindi was different from that of the permanent garrison of the plains. The dour and resolute John Lawrence would preside, but the proceedings would be enlivened by the presence of Herbert Edwardes 'whose cheerfulness,' wrote Sir John Kaye, 'was so unfailing, and whose political wisdom so often glinted out in bright flashes of wit, that the councils of war which were held during that gathering at Rawalpindi were said to be "great fun".' It had been at one of these councils that the telegram was sent containing a pun worthy of General Napier. It was reported that the garrison at Amballa was about to entrench. Probably at the suggestion of John Nicholson's brother Charles, the whist-playing General Anson had been advised:

'Clubs are trumps, not spades. When in doubt play a big one.'

The controversies about the fate of Peshawar and ultimately of the Punjab did not inhibit John Nicholson once he had succeeded Chamberlain in command of the movable column. In early June he was at Amritsar with a force that consisted of the 52nd Queen's Light Infantry, one hundred and eighty-four Punjabi infantry, some irregular sowars and nine guns. Through late June and early July he was disbanding regiments that showed a spirit of mutiny – two at Phillaur, one at Amritsar, a body of cavalry at Sialkot.

The movable column fought an important action on 12 July. During the night of the 10th to 11th they had covered twenty-six miles and reached a point eighteen miles short of their objective, Gurdaspur. Nicholson decided to continue the march by day: the sun was so fierce that the gunners had to cover their carriages and waggons with branches cut down from trees. It was not until 6 o'clock on the evening of the 11th that the force entered Gurdaspur and bivouacked in the little town unobserved by the mutineers.

When it was reported next morning to Nicholson that the mutineers were crossing the Ravi river at Trimmu Ghat about nine miles away, he decided to confront them. The movable column reached Trimmu Ghat at about noon, and there was a fierce action on the banks of the river. About one hundred and twenty mutineers were killed while some were drowned attempting to escape across the river. A party of the rebels, however, managed to make their way to an island taking with them a field gun, but there were no gunners to man it. The piece had been elevated for a long range, and, as the infantry of the movable column advanced upon them, no-one had the presence of mind to depress the screw on the gun, so that its shells flew harmlessly over the heads of Nicholson's men. Throughout that afternoon the rebels on the island were rounded up and later executed by the movable column.

After the battle of the Ravi river Nicholson and his column returned to Amritsar, and from there on 24 July Nicholson was summoned to Lahore to confer with John Lawrence. His orders were to march on Delhi.

The purpose of the movable column was speed. The paraphernalia that surrounded a body of troops on the march was pruned to the minimum. The marches were forced: in one night forty-six miles were covered, and calculated risks must have been taken in the choice of routes. The young ensign Reginald Wilberforce of the 52nd Light Infantry who accompanied Nicholson described the leader and the column. By day Nicholson would often spend hours sitting motionless in his saddle in the burning sun. Part of the column consisted of 'a motley crew called the Multani Horse. They came out of personal devotion to Nicholson, they took no pay from the Government, they recognized no head but Nicholson . . . these men, some two-fifty in number, mounted on their wiry ponies, surrounded the column like a web; they rode in couples, each couple within signalling distance of the other, and so circled the column round for many a mile.' The movable column had left the far north in the last days of July, and reached the camp behind the ridge on 7 August. Nicholson himself had appeared in the camp a few days ahead of his force, and the news of his arrival was like an electric shock. 'Nicholson has come on ahead and is a host in himself,' Hodson wrote in his diary.

Nicholson was attended day and night by 'a huge Pathan, black whiskered and moustachioed', who slept in front of the opening of his tent and stood behind his chair at the mess table with a cocked revolver in his hand. The Brigadier General was as impressive as his body-servant, towering with his six feet two inches over the conventional, mild old men who commanded on the ridge. His 'imperial air . . . which would have been thought arrogance in one of less imposing mien' was soon felt, too, by the British troops. ' "Jack, the general's here," said one. "How do you know?" "Why, look there; there's his mark!" ' And the first trooper pointed to a pair of gallows from each of which dangled six mutineers, while close by were several bullock-carts full of others awaiting their turn.

Chapter Four

ACTIONS AND REACTIONS

'A polished Brahmin or a polished Mohammedan is a savage still.'

At first Nicholson's haughty manner repelled many of the officers on the ridge. His arrival would cast a chill in a mess-tent; a cold douche of aloof disapproval would silence the amiable chatter; the deep sombre eyes seemed to focus on nothing but the military excellence which he sought. Major Reid at first was much put off by the manner of the new arrival, and said so to Baird Smith, who told him: 'Yes, but that wears off; you will like him better when you have seen more of him.' And Reid did; within a week they were the firmest friends.

As soon as he arrived Nicholson examined the whole position on the ridge. 'He was soon passing from picket to picket,' wrote Sir John Kaye, 'taking in with a soldier's eye all the points of our position, and looking down critically upon the defences of the enemy.' On his second day on the ridge he visited the Sirmoor Battalion at Hindu Rao's house. It was Reid's first encounter with the brigadier: 'about this time a visitor of very striking appearance was remarked visiting all our pickets, examining everything and making most searching enquiries about their strength and history. His attire gave no clue to his rank . . .'

Nicholson's position was anomalous. Though he was to assume a *de facto* leadership of all the forces on the ridge, his official position was merely that of the commander of a body of ferocious, bandit-like irregulars, many of them recruited from the tribes of the frontier, with a battalion of European troops attached. Perhaps many thought his force might prove unamenable to the conventional discipline of a civilized army. Certainly the senior officers already on the ridge resented his presence, particularly those from the Queen's regiments. Normally it took years to reach the rank of brigadier – Wilson was considered young to have reached it in his early fifties; and Nicholson was only thirty-five. Moreover, to the conventional, his service seemed to have been of the most dubious kind. Not only was he of the Company's service and not the Queen's but a lot of his soldiering, like Hodson's, had been among the wild tribes, much of it on detachment performing a multitude of tasks – policing, administering his own form of rough-and-ready justice – that could not properly be called soldiering at all; he was sometimes referred to contemptuously as 'Mr Nicholson'.

Nicholson found dissension among the senior officers in the camp. There was an antipathy between Wilson and Baird Smith, and the point of controversy was the strategy of the whole siege. All who knew him testified to Wilson's personal courage, but like Anson, Barnard and Reed before him he placed an undue value on the virtue of prudence. On 20 August he wrote a long memorandum rehearsing once again the dangers of assault with so small a force against so large a garrison of trained soldiers with almost unlimited ammunition for rifles and guns. He pointed out that the whole of the Field Force was barely 12,000, with a large proportion in hospital, and that the defences were reliably estimated at 40,000; that any effective assault must leave their own camp virtually undefended; that the enemy held positions on the ground that lay between the walls and the ridge, and that the ridge itself might be attacked and taken if a large force were engaged in an assault on the city. The policy should be to defend the ridge, to ward off the continual attacks of the mutineers and to consolidate the position, and then to wait for the arrival of a large relieving force.

To this the chief engineer made a spirited reply. An assault should be made as soon as the siege-train had arrived from the north without waiting for further reinforcements of cavalry or infantry. The task, except for the actual capture and occupation of the city, was one for the gunners and sappers. Baird Smith argued that the decision to assault was almost a technical one; and, in a camp where order groups had tended to become debating societies, Baird Smith was supported by some of the most capable officers, by Hodson, Alexander Taylor and Nicholson himself. Wilson, wearily and reluctantly, conceded the point. In a memorandum of the next day he made his points about the need for caution, but ended: 'I yield, however, to the judgment of the Chief Engineer. A.W.'

Conditions in the camp were changing. The rains had come, great torrential downpours that hammered on the canvas of the little conical tents in the lines, that turned the whole camp, as the chaplain Rotton said, into one large pool 'very offensive to the sense of smell'. With the rains came more cholera. By the beginning of August there were eight field hospitals filled for the most part not with casualties of the fighting but with those certain to die of disease. There was no nursing, and two of the surgeons had already been buried. Rotton was tireless. It was physically impossible for him to visit each of the dying men, and so he used to place a stool in the middle of a hospital tent and lead dozens of them in prayer. His beard had grown, his clerical clothes were in tatters, giving him the air of a Corsican bandit. No longer did he need a prayer-book for the burial service: by August, in that swampy, disease-laden camp behind the ridge, he knew it by heart.

But there were recreations for the soldiers who were not in the field hospitals. Some fished in the canals behind the cantonments. There were races with all sort of animals. By late July traders had come down from the north and opened a bazaar among the tents. A friendship had grown up between the men of the 60th Rifles and Reid's Sirmoor battalion of Gurkhas, a traditional alliance that was to last for over a century.

Among the officers there were bizarre contrasts in

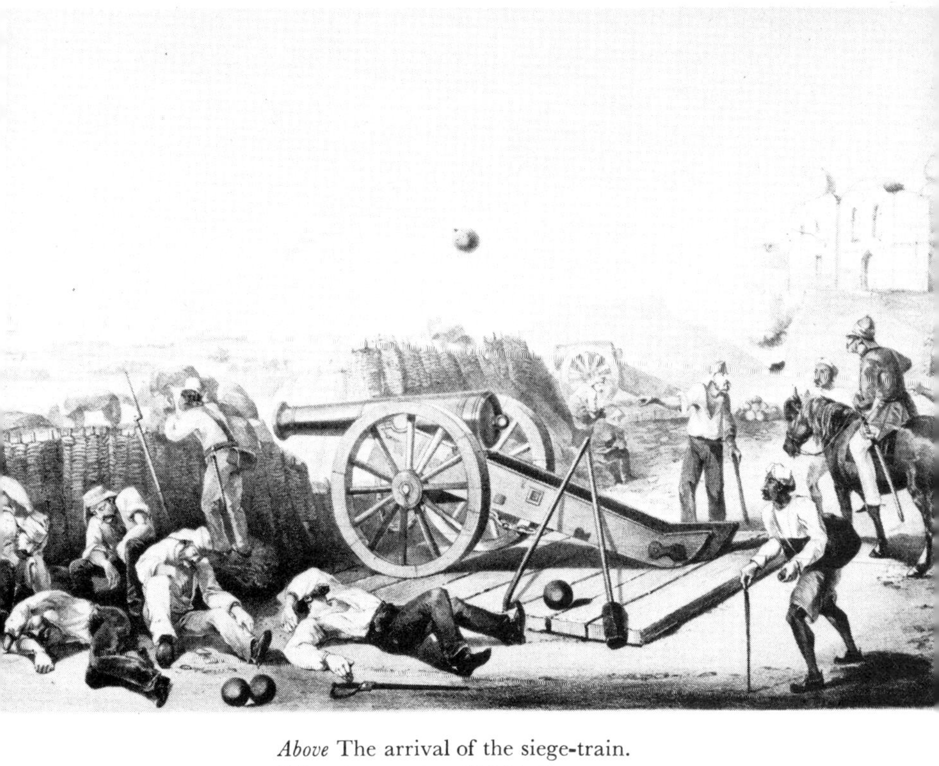

Above The arrival of the siege-train.
Below A scene in a British battery.

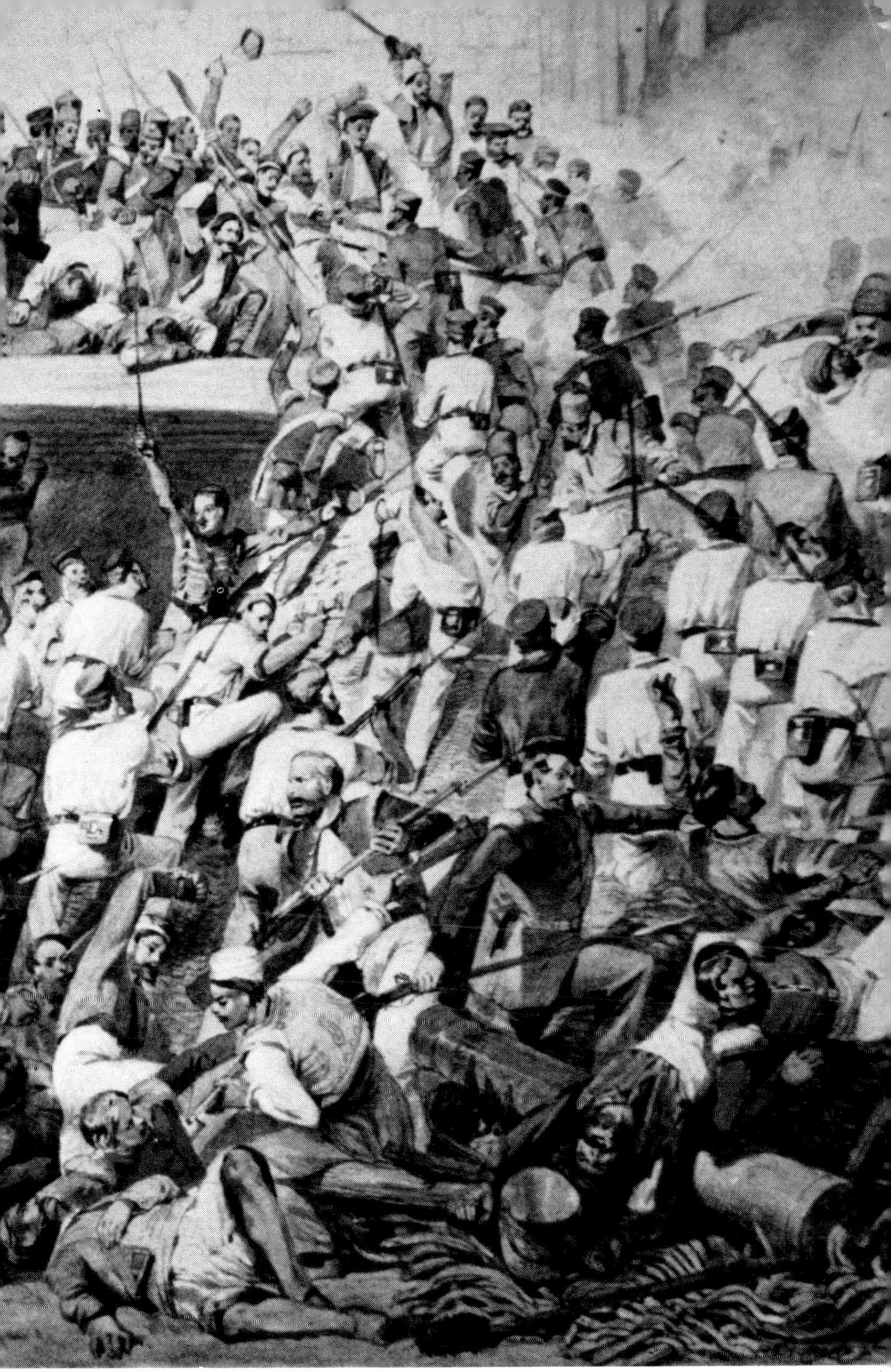

Storming the Kashmir Gate on the morning of 14 September.

Above Major William Hodson leading Hodson's Horse in an action near Delhi early in the Mutiny.
Below Entry through the Kashmir Gate on 14 September.

conditions. In the 60th mess the conventions of that famous regiment were preserved; the officers dressed for dinner in bottle-green and cross-belts; none was allowed to smoke before the table cloth had been removed – not even to steady the nerves when a shell ripped the canvas. The 9th Lancers were punctilious: among swamps, flies and stench they entertained guests and dined off silver. But the hierarchical family structure that binds together an historic regiment was absent in the Headquarters mess; here there was hardly an attempt at appearing in uniforms, and guests were sometimes resented as the food, and more important the drink, was scarce.

The best spirit, perhaps, was in the mess of the Engineers, twenty-two officers under Baird Smith and Alex Taylor, men banded together by a sense of purpose who realized their work was never-ending and essential. Their mess was certainly the most comfortable. They had secured a large house surrounded by a verandah, and adapted a billiards table to dine off. Here the presiding spirit was young Captain Alexander Taylor, who had commanded the Engineers until the arrival of Baird Smith. He was a man of great energy and resource, of great popularity in the camp; and, moreover, an engineer of considerable talent. He had been largely responsible for the building of the Grand Trunk Road.

No officers in the camp worked harder than the engineers. On them depended the construction of the breast-works for defence and the repairing of the batteries. The subalterns – Wilberforce Greathed, Julius Medley, George Chesney – had an exhausting routine when they were engineer duty officers. It began at five in the evening when the out-going duty officer was relieved in the village of Sabsi Mandi, and as soon as night fell a working party under another officer would arrive to spend the night on the defences of the outlying pickets and batteries, for all the work was done under the cover of darkness – it was cooler and safer. Julius Medley on his first tour as duty officer was surprised at the sang-froid of the gunners who were able to snatch fifteen minutes' sleep between firing.

But the morale of the sappers had not always been high. Until he was succeeded by Alexander Taylor the contingent had been commanded by Major Laughton. He had shown no interest in the drawing-up of plans for breaching the Delhi walls and had been glad to delegate most of his duties to the junior officers, spending most of his days and nights in his tent with his demanding Persian wife. Soon she began to complain of the conditions in the camp and then, with a great deal of paraphernalia, left for the comparative safety of the north. It was not until mid-July that Reed felt able to dismiss Laughton from the Field Force: for some reason he was thought to have 'influence' and Barnard had left him alone.

It was Taylor and Baird Smith who repaired the damage done by Laughton, and they had a hard task. The original sapper contingent consisted of five hundred sepoys who had been brought down from Meerut in May, and by early August a large number of these had deserted to the mutineers while others had died of cholera. Baird Smith found only about a hundred who had had the basic training in making trenches and breast-works, in repairing the batteries, constructing gabions and fascines from brushwood. Lawrence had sent some untried Sikhs and pioneers from the north – but these had to be instructed by the officers as they went along. Moreover, the sappers who remained loyal could hear the jeers of their former comrades from within the walls, and the pioneers were distrusted by the Guides and the Gurkhas.

The engineers' 'park' was the most valuable site in the whole camp. Here all their equipment was stored and their numerous pack-animals, mules, elephants, horses, bullocks for the carts, and camels, were quartered. From the 'park' came the ammunition that fed the guns and the mortars in the batteries. It was part ordnance depot, part workshop and part zoo.

The gunners, too, had an exacting task. There were batteries at the exposed, forward position at Metcalfe's house which had been occupied on 12 June to protect the left flank. The centenary of Clive's victory at Plassey on 23 June had been predicted by the fakirs as a day of good omen, and on that day the mutineers mounted a large attack on Metcalfe's and Hindu Rao's house. In this battle some of the gunners dropped down with exhaustion, and the officers took over the lighting of the portfires and the loading. Ammunition, too, had to be conserved, so a reward of half a rupee was paid for each one of the enemy's shot that was retrieved by the camp-followers. Captain Griffiths saw a party of servants coming up the reverse slope of the ridge carrying provisions for the pickets: 'Two round-shot fired by the enemy struck the top of the ridge and rolled down the declivity. Here was a prize worth contending for, and the cooks, depositing the dishes on the ground, ran in all haste to seize the treasures.' But they forgot that the shot had not had time to cool, and the two who won the race 'picked up the balls, and, uttering a cry, dropped them quickly, rubbing and blowing their hands. The remainder stood patiently waiting, and then, after a time, spent evidently in deliberation, two men placed the shot on their heads, and all in a body moved off towards the Commissariat quarters to receive and divide the reward.'

Once the mutineers actually penetrated the camp. This was on 9 July. They tried to persuade some gunners to desert their posts and join them; when persuasion failed, they killed them. Harriet Tytler, who was with her baby in the Bell of Arms, heard it all. The enemy unlimbered the guns of the sepoys they had killed and 'sent the horses galloping through the camp with all their trappings clattering behind them.' The alarm was given and the men turned out 'some with shirt-sleeves tucked up, others without shoes or socks, just as they had turned out of bed when off duty.' The enemy were engaged outside the cantonment cemetery and beaten off, leaving forty dead. 'I shall never forget the sight,' wrote Harriet Tytler, 'the glistening of the bayonets even through the smoke.'

Through those terrible summer months – when at first the dry hot air was black with flies, and then, when the rains came, boots and clothing were covered in a green mildew – alarming news from other parts of India was reaching the force on the ridge. There was the panic in Calcutta. There had been a fear that mutineers were descending on the capital and many tried to flee, blocking the streets with horse-drawn carriages; and, as Kaye wrote, from those parts of the capital 'occupied mainly by the great world of clerkdom . . . the exodus is described as universal.' The mutiny at Meerut and the fall of Delhi were followed by mutinies throughout the Gangetic plain, the defection of a whole brigade at the garrison town of Bareilly, the besieging of the Europeans at Neemuch.

By the end of June there was terrible news from Cawnpore. Here the garrison was commanded by Sir Hugh Wheeler, an experienced veteran married to an Indian. He seems to have made two cardinal mistakes. The first was to permit a deplorable unpreparedness in the defences and to do little to keep up morale. An officer commanding a relief party from Lucknow to Cawnpore noted: 'I saw quite enough to convince me that if any insurrection took or takes place, we shall have no one to thank but ourselves, because we have now shown the natives how easily we can become frightened, and when frightened utterly helpless.' Wheeler's second error was to believe in the friendliness of the Nana Sahib whose court at Bithur was close to the garrison town. Mutiny broke out on 5 June and for three weeks the Europeans were besieged. At the end of the month the Europeans were offered a safe passage by the Nana Sahib, in small craft in the river Ganges. The women and children were removed to the Bibighur in the city and butchered with indescribable ferocity on the eve of Cawnpore's relief, the corpses being then thrown down a well.

When the relieving party entered Cawnpore the full horrors were revealed. Sergeant Forbes-Mitchell of the 93rd Highlanders saw the slaughter-house. 'The floors of the rooms were still covered with congealed blood,' he wrote, 'littered with trampled, torn dresses of women and children, shoes, slippers and locks of long hair.' Most terrible of all he saw a hook in the wall from which a child had been hung: 'all round the hook on a level with it was covered with the handprints, and below the hook with the footprints, in blood, of a little child.' The sergeant examined the well where the bodies had been thrown, and saw also some of the dreadful vengeance. In front of the slaughter-house a gallows had been erected by the relieving force. 'During my stay,' wrote Forbes Mitchell, those wretches were hanged, after having been flogged, and each made to clean about a square foot of the blood from the floor of the house.'

When the news of the massacre reached the ridge there was at first a stupefied and shocked dejection. To raise the spirits of those in the lines Wilson ordered a regimental band to play daily in the centre of the camp. But the stupefaction changed in many to a cold and sometimes indiscriminate hatred. There were those now resolved to give full vent to their instinct for retribution, who now distrusted any Indians, even the faithful among the camp-followers, the water-carriers and the coolies who fed the guns with ammunition. The massacre at Cawnpore was the most terrible of the whole rebellion; it was to be avenged by the slaughter within the walls of Delhi. There was enthusiasm among many for the harshness of Colonel Neill after the recapture of Cawnpore, agreement with Havelock's dictum 'that severity at the first is mercy in the end', and approval for the detailed orders for executing the murderers that the General gave: 'each miscreant, after sentence of death is pronounced upon him, will be taken down to the house in question, under a guard, and will be forced into cleaning up a small portion of the bloodstains: the task will be made as revolting to his feelings as possible, and the Provost-Marshal will use the lash into forcing anyone objecting to complete his task. After properly cleaning up his portion the culprit is to be immediately hanged . . .'

Reactions to the massacre caused a reversal of public opinion in England and America. On the centenary of the battle of Plassey, while the mutineers from Delhi were mounting an attack on Metcalfe's house and the right flank of the ridge, a meeting in London celebrating Clive's victory could be told that 'the late defection in the Indian Army' had been caused by a departure from the spirit of Clive, which had been 'to treat the sepoys, not with severity, but with kindness.' This was a reversal of the truth: the mutiny was caused not by the harshness, but by the relaxation of discipline in the sepoy army.

By the beginning of the next month reports were being printed in the London newspapers of the atrocities, some exaggerated and some without foundation, of children being impaled in front of their mothers, of unmentionable assaults on European women. These last were almost certainly false accusations against the mutineers: Sir William Muir, chief of the Intelligence Department of the North-West Province disbelieved the stories that European women had been raped. 'The colour,' he remarked, 'is repugnant to the Oriental taste', and that indignities had been inflicted not 'from the lust of desire', but to 'bring shame and degradation on the English name.'

By the middle of July few in England would have referred to the mutiny as 'the late defections in India'. After the news of the murder of the Christians in Delhi and the massacre on the Ganges and in the Bibighur a cry for vengeance went up. The Nana Sahib, once a popular figure, was execrated; the well became a symbol of dark deeds in dark places. All this annoyed Lord Canning. He deplored what he referred to as the 'rabid and indiscriminate vindictiveness', and that not one man in ten questioned the fact that 'the hanging and shooting of 40,000 or 50,000 men can be otherwise than practicable and right.' The Queen, too, was disturbed by 'the un-Christian spirit shown also to a great extent here by the public towards India in general.' 'Clemency' Canning, as he was now contemptuously dubbed, was for checking the blood-lust that was spreading like an epidemic, fastest, it was noted, in the safest places, like the hill-stations and the garrison towns protected by European troops.

To many Canning was the symbol of the hesitancy and weakness that had partially caused the mutiny and then failed to check its course. Now he appeared to be advocating a policy of misplaced leniency, sometimes amounting to a denial of justice itself. The superstitious saw his assumption of office as accompanied by bad omens: he was the thirteenth Governor-General; as he mounted the steps of Government House on his arrival he had stumbled and nearly fallen; there was his pessimism and his well-known and publicized premonitions of disaster during his reign. Surely, thought many in England and in the hill-stations and garrison towns of India, the stern justice of Havelock, Neill and Nicholson was to be preferred to the 'clemency' of Canning?

In fact all that Canning was advocating was discrimination. He issued instructions in July for the putting down of lawlessness and the restoration of order by the military in districts where 'the civil authority has been entirely overthrown'. This should be done 'with such promptitude and severity as will strike terror into the minds of the evil disposed . . .' and should be calculated 'to induce them by fear of death to abstain from plunder.' But once order was restored there should be no reprisals. This might lead Indians to 'band together in large numbers . . . with a view to retaliation' which would 'greatly add to the difficulties of settling the country : . .'

In India there was an outcry against the attitude of the Governor-General. In August a petition signed by nearly seven hundred European citizens of Calcutta was sent to the Queen asking for Canning's removal from office. It asserted that the disasters were 'directly attributable to the blunders, weakness and incapacity of the local Government of India of which the present Governor-General is the responsible head.' The petitioners attacked Canning's 'feebleness and vacillation' and his 'ill-timed and hopeless policy of conciliation'. These sentiments were echoed in the press in India. 'Laxity towards any portion of the conspirators is misplaced, impolitic and iniquitous,' ran a leading article commenting on

Canning's instructions, 'and is calculated to excite contempt and invite attack on every side . . .' Even Cardinal Wiseman in a pastoral letter trumpeted forth against those who had 'not merely resumed the barbarity of their ancient condition, but borrowed the ferocity of the tiger in his jungle, to torture, to mutilate, to antagonize, and to destroy.' And the Bishop of Oxford declared at a meeting of the Society for the Propagation of the Gospel that 'a polished Brahmin or a polished Mohammedan is a savage still.'

Disraeli, the most eloquent of his party in opposition to the Liberal government of Lord Palmerston, was the advocate of moderation. He told his constituents in Buckinghamshire (where so many of the soldiers of the 52nd Light Infantry, then defending the ridge, were recruited) that he wanted retributive justice against the mutineers who had committed atrocities in Delhi and Cawnpore, but that he deplored the hysterical demands for general vengeance on the population of India. 'The horrors of war need no stimulant. The horrors of war, carried on as the war in India is at present, especially want no stimulant . . . I protest against meeting atrocities by atrocities.' He had, he said, heard and read things that made him 'suppose that the religious opinions of the people of England had undergone some sudden change; and that instead of bowing before the name of Jesus, we were preparing to revive the worship of Moloch.'

On the ridge in mid-August the torrential downpours continued. Baird Smith had been badly wounded in the ankle and limped about the camp unable to wear a boot but tireless in his inspection of the breast-works, sitting up in his damp and mildewed tent poring over his plans of assault by the light of a hurricane lamp. Nicholson now had the habit of climbing the rickety stairs to Major Reid's headquarters at the top of Hindu Rao's house, and was gratified to find that he was always challenged by alert Gurkha sentries when he approached. Hodson was in charge of intelligence, and, as Colonel Seaton wrote: 'spies came in from the city at all times during the day, and in all sorts of disguises, some bearing intelligence by word of mouth, others bringing mysterious little scrolls that had been concealed in the most inexplicable manner.'

Wilson had received a sharp letter from the Governor-General asking why an attack on Delhi was so long delayed, so after his exchange of memoranda with Baird Smith he called on the Chief Engineer, and the two men amicably and seriously discussed a plan of assault. It was to take place early in September, despite the heat and the rains, and without waiting for the massive reinforcements that Wilson wanted, which were now unlikely ever to arrive as Havelock and his army were besieging Lucknow. Relations between Baird Smith and Wilson were better, now that the General had at last been persuaded of the necessity for attack; but Baird Smith could still write to his wife that he was 'beginning to suspect that Wilson has a good deal of the dame in him. He so prefers small designs and incomplete conceptions to doing anything thorough . . .', and Nicholson had set his mind firmly against the commander, with a contempt for Wilson that was to last until the walls had been breached and Nicholson was dying in his tent. 'I have seen lots of useless generals in my day,' he declared, 'but such an ignorant, croaking obstructive as he is, I have never hitherto met with; and nothing will induce me to serve a day under his personal command after the fall of this place.'

At the end of the month, however, there was to be the chance of action for Nicholson, action approved by the hesitant commander of the Delhi Field Force. A second, larger and essential siege-train – better than the 'trumpery affair' that had arrived in camp a few weeks before – was being put together in the north and was eagerly awaited in the camp. To secure its safe arrival it was decided to strike at the enemy forces believed to be holding positions north of the cantonments. The siege-train itself was escorted only by a small detachment of sepoys, and, through observation and Hodson's spies, it was learnt that the mutineers were sending a large force northwards to intercept it.

At dawn on 25 August Nicholson left camp with a force of 1,600 infantry and 450 cavalry. Some of the best officers of the Delhi Field Force were with him: there was Major Tombs and his troop of horse artillery that had contributed so much to the victories on the Hindun in June; there was Charles Griffiths and men of the 61st Queen's regiment, and young Edward Vibart; Sir Theophilus Metcalfe accompanied the force as a guide, and Hodson of course had been anxious to join, but his health had broken and he was confined by the regimental surgeon to his tent with dysentery.

Nicholson thought that the intercepting force of mutineers was making for the village of Bahadurgarh. The only route to it was a rough bullock track with swamps and bogs on either side. The infantry at times waded waist-high with ammunition and arms carried overhead, and the track itself proved impassable for the field artillery. The guns got stuck in mud up to the axles, and it took the expedition seven hours to reach a village nine miles to the north of the camp. Nicholson's scouts reported that the enemy were not at the village of Bahadurgarh but in a position, still twelve miles further on, protected by a right-angled fork of the Najafgarh Jheel.

At 4 o'clock in the afternoon the enemy's position was sighted, and it appeared to be a strong one. To the front they held a small walled 'serai' with four field guns, partially protected by rising ground. Behind this there were two small villages, each occupied in strength by infantry and protected in front by artillery. To their right was a cluster of houses occupied by infantry. The whole position was protected in the rear by the deep canal, the Najafgarh Jheel, and on the enemy's left by a wide, swampy ditch fordable in one place. The strength of the enemy was estimated at six thousand, nearly four times Nicholson's force.

By the afternoon the British force was exhausted. Sixteen miles had been covered in about twelve hours, miles of swamp and mud, for the most part in a torrential downpour. But Nicholson was determined on an immediate attack such as the movable column had made a month before on the Ravi river.

The attack was to be mounted first on what Nicholson, after his quick reconnaissance, thought to be the enenmy's strongest point, the serai. This is how he addressed the men of the 61st Queen's regiment: 'You all know what Sir Colin Campbell said to you at Chillianwalla, and you must also have heard that he used a similar expression at the battle of the Alma, that is – "Hold your fire till within twenty or thirty yards of that battery, and then, my boys, we will make short work of it." '

Having forded the ditch on the enemy's left flank – waist-high in water – the infantry were ordered down by Nicholson who, however, remained himself, alone and exposed, in front of them to observe the position in the serai. Tombs' artillery began their bombardment and under cover of this the infantry advanced in a line a hundred yards long, with fixed bayonets, to the walls of the enemy position. Nicholson himself obeyed the advice of Sir Colin Campbell and did not give the order to charge until the line was almost thirty yards from the walls, and then his harsh voice could be heard over the field of battle, above the hissing of the shot and the crash of the mortars. 'In less time than it takes to relate,' wrote Edward Vibart, 'we had scaled the walls, carried the serai, and captured all the guns . . .'

With shouts and cheers the infantry tumbled into the serai. Mutineers were bayonetted while still loading with the very cartridges against which they had rebelled only four months before. Then, with the loss of their thirteen guns, a great deal of ammunition and treasure that they had looted, they fled in confusion from the little walled village. But the baggage of Nicholson's force was still far behind on the swampy road from Delhi, and the victorious soldiers were compelled to spend the night without tents, soaked to the skin. Charles Griffiths described it with understatement as 'supremely uncomfortable'. This, the greatest victory since the battle for Badli-ke-Serai, had cost few in casualties – twenty-five killed, seventy wounded and twenty horses lost. Among the killed was an 18-year-old lieutenant in the 61st, Elkington. He seems to have had a premonition of his death. Usually vivacious and talkative he had been silent on the long march from the camp, and when his effects were examined after the force arrived back behind the ridge, his friends noticed that they had been carefully parcelled up and instructions left for their disposal.

The whole camp turned out to greet Nicholson's force on its return. The bands played and the last part of their route was lined by soldiers, cheering and waving their caps. Congratulations for Nicholson poured in. John Lawrence wrote that if he had had the authority he would have knighted him on the spot. Archdale Wilson issued an order of the day on 'the glorious results of the Najafgarh expedition' and commending Nicholson's 'judgment, energy and determination'. Enemy losses were reckoned at five hundred, but most important of all their guns had been captured, and this was the token of victory. The road was now open for the arrival of the siege-train from the north: when that arrived, an attempt could be made to breach the walls of the city. After the battle of Najafgarh, Sir John Kaye wrote, 'there was not a soldier in camp who did not then feel that the time of waiting and watching had well-nigh passed . . .'

The siege-train, drawn by elephants, arrived on 4 September. It consisted of twenty-four heavy guns and mortars and with it came ammunition and stores. Within the next three days there were also reinforcements: on the same day as the siege-train there arrived another four hundred European soldiers and the Baluchi battalion, who appeared to Charles Griffiths 'a most savage-looking lot of men'. On the 7th came a contingent of Sikh cavalry sent by the Rajah of Jhind who had kept open the British lines of communication to the north. On the same day came Wilde's regiment of Punjabis – seven hundred of them – and a contingent of over two thousand with four guns sent by the Maharajah of Kashmir.

When this massive reinforcement of men, guns and stores had arrived in camp there was a final council of war. Young

Frederick Roberts was on Nicholson's staff, and this cheerful, modest subaltern had succeeded in penetrating the reserve of his awe-inspiring superior. Before the council Roberts was with Nicholson in his tent, and even at this late hour the Brigadier thought it possible that Wilson might draw back and not order an assault. Nicholson talked to Roberts 'in confidential terms of personal matters' ending by saying that unless the council agreed to assault he would be prepared to take 'a very unusual step', and was prepared to propose at the meeting that Wilson be superseded. Roberts said that he was 'greatly startled': this action would have been totally at variance with the customs of the service, an act of insubordination, almost of mutiny, in itself. Roberts pointed out to Nicholson that as the Adjutant-General Neville Chamberlain was wounded and out of action, he, Nicholson, was the next in seniority to Wilson. Nicholson smiled, and answered: 'I have not overlooked that fact . . . I could not possibly accept the command myself, and I shall propose that it be given to Campbell of the 52nd; I am prepared to serve under him for the time being, so that no one can ever accuse me of being influenced by personal motives.'

Roberts walked with Nicholson to the Headquarters tent and waited for his chief in great excitement while the council was in progress. When it was over and Nicholson emerged, he learnt to his relief that Wilson had agreed to an immediate assault on the walls, that there was no need of any 'very unusual step'. But clearly Wilson was beginning to crack and this was noticed with a certain sympathy by Baird Smith, though with none at all by Nicholson. Letters from the General poured in for the Chief Engineer at the rate of four, five and six a day. Sometimes they were peevish: 'I have already more than I can manage, and my head gets into such a state that I feel nearly mad sometimes. For God's sake, don't make me quite so . . .' And nearly always discouraging: '. . . I cannot suggest any other plan to meet our difficulties . . . The chances of success under such a heavy fire as the working-parties will be exposed to are anything but favourable.'

Baird Smith's patience ran out, and at last this busy man ignored the tiresome memoranda from his general. 'He is so peevish and positively childish,' he wrote. 'He combines a wondrous amount of ignorance and obstinacy, is so discouraging, has such a total want of vim and energy that he is literally the greatest obstacle extant in the vigorous capture of Delhi.'

It was not only Baird Smith, Alexander Taylor and the engineers who were working all hours of the day and night during the week before the assault. The artillery were organizing an artillery park for the overhauling and maintenance of the guns and the storing of ammunition. The guns of the siege-train had been drawn into camp by elephants, but elephants cannot be trusted under fire, and the gun-carriages had to be adapted so that they could be drawn to the batteries by bullocks. All this was undertaken by Colonel Hogge who had come into camp ahead of the siege-train. And all this was the immediate priority: the assault was to begin with a long, sustained barrage from the artillery.

Before the barrage could begin surveys had to be made of the terrain between the ridge and the walls. The Field Force's maps were inadequate, and it fell to Alexander Taylor to make good the deficiency. The surveys had to be done in secret; much of the ground that Taylor needed to study was still occupied by the mutineers. Soon Taylor found that there was a technical problem to be overcome. So well had the British engineers done their work half a century before that the escarpment was so positioned that if a shot cleared it, it would normally be too high to do any damage to the curtain of wall. After many dangerous patrols, Taylor found that if the artillery aimed at an angle, firing at a bastion's flank, the shots would strike low and would prove effective. It was these patrols that determined the positioning of the crucial no. 1 and no. 2 batteries which were to demolish the enemy's bastions at the north-western section of the Delhi walls.

At the time that Taylor was making his surveys the enemy held Ludlow Castle, but their occupation of it was only spasmodic. There were long periods of time between one picket of mutineers leaving and the arrival of their relief. On one expedition Taylor, armed only with a pistol and accompanied by a small escort of Guides, reached Ludlow Castle, penetrated below it to the gardens of the Kudsia Bagh, and was able to make his calculations, unobserved by an enemy sentry who was only a few yards away.

On another of these reconnaissance expeditions Taylor and a subaltern, Charles Thomason, were confronted by two hundred mutineers manning one of the walls of the Kudsia Bagh. A volley was fired and, as the mutineers ducked behind the wall to re-load, Thomason remarked that he and Taylor could not take Delhi single-handed. 'But don't let's run,' said Taylor. So the two young officers walked calmly back to the shelter of a gully and then, as Thomason wrote later, 'once out of sight we put our heads down and legged it as fast as we could along the stream-bed.'

The target for the artillery was the northernmost part of the city's defences, at that part of the curtain of wall by the Kashmir Gate, the Moree Bastion and the position known as the Water Bastion. On 7 September howitzers, field guns and mortars from the batteries on the ridge and at Metcalfe's house broke the gentle noises of dawn with the first deafening salvo, and a pall of smoke rose slowly into the still air.

Chapter Five

DEFENDERS

'The splendour of the sovereignty of Delhi will again revive.'

On the evening of 11 May, when the city had been in the hands of the mutineers for half a day, the 54th Native Infantry occupied and prepared to defend the Selimgarh Fort, jutting out into the slow-moving river to the north of the palace. During the night, wrote a citizen of Delhi, a twenty-one gun salute was fired from the fort, which caused a panic as many thought it was the British on their way to assault: 'the greatest uneasiness and tumult continued to prevail in consequence of the plunder, pillage and burning of houses.' The Delhi College was burned: Ram Chandra, a professor of the college, a convert to Christianity and an advocate of women's education, was rescued and hidden by his Moslem brother. Others were less fortunate. Some Christians were dragged from their houses and killed, others were slain as they made for the Jumna and the supposed safety of its eastern bank. In all forty-nine Christians, mostly women, were rounded up, to be massacred on the 16th.

The King seems to have tried to prevent the massacre. The interpreter Jeewan Lall reported that he had ordered the sepoys to separate themselves into two parties, Moslems and Hindus, and then had 'appealed to each to consult their religious advisers to see if there were any authority for the slaughter of helpless men, women and children.' His pleas were unavailing, and while the butchery was in progress 'the King and his assembled counsellors stood like dumb puppets.'

The massacre of the Christians was the climax to five days of pillage. Jeewan Lall wrote that on the night of 11 – 12 May the respectable citizens of each neighbourhood 'were occupied in arranging for the watch and ward', and the police officer, Maniodin, approached the King to plead with him to recruit a force to restrain the more indisciplined of the sepoys and to check the plundering of the badmashes. From midday on the 11th all the shops were closed, and when Maniodin returned after the fall of the city he found the centre deserted; Jeewan Lall noticed the barricaded doors of the shops, 'the inmates concealed inside sitting silent in terror, or praying to God for His mercy and protection.' A group of rich citizens clubbed together and paid for one of the regiments to protect their houses; but the shahzadas, princes of the blood, heard of it and brought the arrangement to an end, at the same time imposing a fine on the paymasters.

But on the first day after the seizure of the city all was triumph. For the first time in fifteen years a durbar, a royal public ceremony, was held. The King sat on a silver throne in the Diwan-i-Khas, the hall of public audience. There was a review of the sepoys from Meerut and Delhi, a salute of guns was fired, and Mahbub Ali Khan the minister was ordered to give a feast for the whole army. The sepoys were issued with sticky, sweet confectionery and their officers with a present of money. Two grocers, Ram Sabai and Dilwani Mal, were directed to supply food to the value of 500 rupees a day for the needs of the 'bahadshi', the King of Delhi's army. Then the King, perched in a howdah that swayed with the rhythm of the elephant's pace, was taken in procession through his city, while at beat of drum a proclamation was read calling on the traders to open their shops.

At first, however, the King was powerless to restore order. 'I am helpless,' he told Maniodin; 'all my attendants have lost their heads or fled. I have no force to obey my orders: what can I do?' The police officer had ridden to the cantonments abandoned by the British. Here he found 'the whole place in disorder; ruins of burning bungalows, and remains of property scattered here and there.' All the mutinous sepoy regiments had moved from the cantonments into the centre of the capital.

The initative in these days was not with the King. He appears to have been bewildered by events for twenty-four hours. His first action was to send a messenger with an appeal for help to the Lieutenant-Governor at Agra. His immediate reaction when the sowars crossed the bridge of boats and demonstrated under the balcony of his palace was to call on them to disperse. Moreover the vazir, Mahbub Ali Khan, had fallen ill with dropsy on the eve of the mutiny, and his place had in effect been taken by the hakim, the court physician, Ahsan Ullah Khan, a man of tact and moderation and one who was to play an ambiguous role in Delhi during the siege. Temperamentally the hakim seems to have been at odds with the King. At first he advised the King to disown the mutineers, then to try to come to terms with the British. Then the King, realizing that Delhi had been stripped of all foreign control, and probably at the insistence of his own sons, threw in his lot with the mutineers. Appeals were made to the princes of northern India – some, like the Maharajah of Patiala, merely forwarded the King's letter without comment to the British authorities. At the durbar on 12 May a firman was issued calling on all Moslems and Hindus to join the revolt, and to copy out the words of the proclamation and post it in public places.

Ahsan Ullah Khan was continually suspected of being a traitor, and his house was ransacked by a mob. Even the King seems to have had his doubts about the hakim's loyalty. 'Why should the treatment of my indisposition be not disagreeable,' ran one of his Persian quatrains, 'for my physician bears goodwill to my enemies?' But the King had one trait that saved Ahsan Ullah Khan again and again; it was a loyalty, sometimes quixotic, to his court and his servants.

It was Ahsan Ullah Khan and the ailing Mahbub Ali Khan who, during the middle of May, headed the administration of the city and set up the instruments of government. Theoretically Moslem law prevailed, but there was no attempt at returning to early forms of administration. The titles, the etiquette, were all Persian; the methods were British. There was to be a council for the city of ten members. There was to be, and this was to have greater power, a military court composed of two officers each from the infantry, the cavalry and the artillery, as well as four civilian members. This court was to elect a chairman, to supervise the daily running of the city, to control the supply of food, to advise on the defences of the walls and the fort, and most important of all to try to raise funds to support the swelling numbers of the bahadshi.

Then there were the conferences, almost every day, at the Diwan-i-Khas, where the King sat enthroned, issued instructions and gave rewards, mediated between the quarrelling princes and tried to persuade the rich to contribute in money or kind towards the cost of his army. The King seems to have been as much concerned with etiquette as with the fate of soldiers and citizens. Early on he complained that, whereas even senior British officers had dismounted when they entered the walls of the palace, 'these sepoys come riding on horseback . . . while they are under-dressed and wear no turbans on their heads.' Orders were issued to exclude all armed men from the hall of public audience; and, wrote Jeewan Lall, 'youths without turbans were also to be excluded, as being both distasteful and disrespectful to the King.'

One of the King's sons was appointed Commander-in-Chief. This was Mirza Mogul, and he was to prove a disappointment. In his capacity as a link between the military and the civilians he was the recipient of a stream of instructions from his father. It was another, younger, son, Mirza Abu Bakr, who commanded the troops that confronted Archdale Wilson's force from Meerut at the Hindun river. The prince took up a position on the roof of a house to watch the battle, but after a shell burst close to him 'he hastily descended . . . mounted his horse, and galloped off with his escort of sowars far into the rear of the position, not heeding the cries of his troops.' On their return to the gates of the city this Plaza-Toro and his troops were jeered, and the prince was shortly relieved of his command.

On 19 May a sinister proclamation appeared on the walls of the Jumma Masjid. It came from the Maulvi Muhammad Sayyid and called for a 'jehad' or holy war, not against the feringi only, but against the Hindus. At the end of May, pressure for such a war had grown, and the King proclaimed, at beat of drum through the streets of the capital, that rivalry between Hindu and Moslem should cease. Meanwhile, wrote Jeewan Lall, 'the Hindus have closed all their houses for fear of their lives.'

It was not only strife between Hindu and Moslem with which the King and the military court had to contend. On 28 May quarrels broke out between the sepoys from Delhi and the original mutineers from Meerut, one group accusing the other of profiting from the plunder and pillage. The sowars from Meerut were even accused of having been untrue to their salt and murdering their officers.

But on 2 July there was a great turning-point for the defenders of Delhi, whose morale, after the first days of victory and euphoria, had been growing lower. Mutinous regiments from Bareilly and the Rohilkand marched across the bridge of boats and, in the full view of the British force encamped on the ridge, entered the city with their bands playing, their colours displayed, and singing 'Cheer, boys, cheer!' a popular marching song that they had learnt from the British troops. They consisted of four regiments of infantry, one of cavalry, a battery of horse artillery and two post guns. But most important they brought with them a new commander, who was to supplant the discredited Mirza Mogul, one well known to the British officers, a subadar of artillery called Mahommed Bakht Khan.

Bakht Khan had served the East India Company for forty years, had commanded a battery of field artillery in the first Afghan war, then had served at Neemuch and was a subadar at Bareilly on the outbreak of the mutiny. He was well known to many of the British gunner officers, wrote Captain Forrest, who described him as 'a big fat man, obsequious, fond of the society of Europeans, and very intelligent.' This elderly, corpulent and able leader claimed to be of royal blood. He 'pointed out that he was the descendant of the same family as the King of Delhi,' wrote Jeewan Lall, 'and asked the King to satisfy himself that this was true.'

Royal or not, Bakht Khan's capacities were soon proved. He began regular tours of the city; he inspected the magazine and the factory, soon to employ over two hundred men, for the making of ammunition; and he ordered his troops to assist in the crucial task of collecting revenue. What he found in the royal capital at first must have appalled him. There was despondency: 'there is no arrangement for any provisions, much less for anything else,' a correspondent wrote to the Rajah of Kapurthala. Many of the shops, particularly those of the Hindus, were shuttered and barred, despite the daily appeals of the King to open them. Many thought, as the correspondent wrote to the Rajah, that 'the civilization of fifty-three years has been destroyed in three days.'

There had been a depressing record of defeats. Twice, with ignominy, the royal troops had been thrown back into Delhi from the Hindun river. On 9 June there had been an abortive attempt to dislodge the Field Force from the ridge – the attempt had to be abandoned, and this in full view of many of the citizens of Delhi watching the skirmishes from the roofs of their houses. Much of the ground between the ridge and the walls had been lost and, thought Jeewan Lall, if the British had pressed on they could have entered through the gates. The defeats had added to the lawlessness, and after Ghazi-ud-din-Nagar the King had had to post troops in the bazaars. There had been a slight boost to the spirits of the population, however, when the heads of some Europeans killed in the fighting were hacked off, impaled on pikes and paraded through the streets.

The new Commander-in-Chief found, too, a witch-hunt against spies and traitors. On 8 July five butchers were caught at the gates taking meat to the English camp, and they had their throats cut. Earlier one 'Buldeo Singh . . . was seized and brought to the Kotwali. He was accused of sympathizing with the English. He was shot, and his body suspended from a tree. Thirteen bakers residing at the Kabul Gate were dragged from their houses and killed, on being suspected of supplying bread to the English.' A man had been caught digging a tunnel in a house within the walls of the palace. He was falsely supposed to be in league with the British, and was blown away from a gun at the Selimgarh Fort – 'as a warning to others', as Jeewan Lall grimly commented.

The witch-hunt was the pretext for plundering on the part of the sepoys. 'On the false pretence that an Englishman is lurking inside,' the King complained in a letter to Mirza Mogul, 'they dash into the peoples' private dwellings and plunder them; they break open the locks and take away the shutters and doors and they plunder the goods in the interior most shamelessly.' The King had even considered moving all troops from the Red Fort and the centre of the city and forming camps outside the walls in order to protect the citizens. Residents of the suburb of Pahaganj sent a petition to the King complaining that 'the royal forces coming out of the Ajmer Gate spread in different directions in our bazaar and carried away everything from shops and houses, including bedding, clothes, utensils.' Just before they were relieved of their commands in the army, Bakht Khan 'informed the King that if any of the princes attempted to plunder the city, he would cut off their noses and ears.' The King, weary of the endless petitions from householders and shopkeepers, made no objection.

There had been other complaints, too, about the conduct of the shahzadas. The wife of one of them complained on 5 July to the King that Abu Bakr, who had so failed to distinguish himself at the Hindun river a month before, 'in a state of intoxication, came to her house with several sowars to seize her, and fired several shots with rifles and pistols, and beat a number of people of the Mohalla.'

But it was not the fear of the shopkeepers or the behaviour of his numerous relations that proved the greatest problem to the King and the court of administration. Many of the sepoys had originally mutinied because they considered that they had not been paid what was due to them by the Company. They, the soldiers of the bahadshi, were what they had been as soldiers of the Raj, mercenaries. Their first action in most of the towns in revolt had been attacks on the treasuries. The King was faced with embarrassment over pay. As early as 23 May he ordered appropriations from the bankers; again and again money was wheedled or demanded from the rich in the audiences in the Diwan-i-Khas. The King himself offered to give all his treasures to be melted down for currency. Then, bewildered and exasperated by it all, he declared that all he wanted was to make his way to Mecca as a pilgrim in the robes of a mendicant.

During the months of siege the mood inside the great walls of the capital was a mixture of euphoria, patriotism, avarice, the desire for vengeance, the fear of reprisals. There were acts of sustained bravery on the part of the sepoys, particularly the gunners under their leader Kuli Khan, who was publicly thanked by the King. There was the daring and nearly successful attack on the British right flank from the village of Sabsi Mandi, the attempt to intercept the siege-train that ended at the battle of the Najafgarh Jheel, the sudden and courageous battle in the lines of the British troops. By the sepoys defending the walls and those on the nightly skirmishing parties the immediate cause of it all was forgotten: greased cartridges in their thousands were fired – even after a factory to make ammunition had been set up by order of the King.

What were the defenders fighting for? Ahsan Ullah Khan giving evidence at the King's trial had few illusions: they were fighting, he thought, for loot. If, he declared, the sepoys had been inspired by a yearning for religious and political freedom 'they would not have plundered the houses and property of the people, nor would they have oppressed and injured them, but would have fought only against the British Government.' Another witness, one Sitaram Bawa, was careful to draw a distinction between the sepoys and the badmashes who joined them. 'It is not the brahmins and great men that have destroyed helpless children, women with child and poor women,' he declared with emotion. 'It was the intention to destroy your men, but it was villagers and savages who destroyed your women and children . . .'

Certainly for months before the events in mid-May at Meerut and Delhi there had been plots and mutinous correspondence in the regiments of the Bengal army. Ahsan Ullah Khan bore witness: the 38th Native Infantry at Delhi, he said, had contacted the garrison at Meerut 'so that from every cantonment troops would arrive at Delhi.' When the city fell on the 11th the King of course vacillated, as did his most intimate adviser. But the sepoys acted at once. Letters were sent to the sepoys of other regiments asking for help: 'so many of us have come in here, do you also according to your promise.' There was collusion about resistance to the greased cartridges. Thus a sepoy in Amritsar could write to a sepoy of a sister regiment in Rawalpindi: 'We have on this occasion quitted the service, and seen all with our own eyes. We have written this to you for your information. If you should receive these cartridges, intermarriage, and eating and drinking in common, shall cease between yourselves and us.'

The idea, however, that there was a general plan, well-matured, for a simultaneous uprising of the sepoy regiments in northern India (31 May is the date that has been put forward), and that the revolt at Meerut was premature and thwarted these plans, is probably false. No-one at the trial of the King alleged that there was a definite and co-ordinated plan with the Nana Sahib, the former King of Oudh or the Rani of Jhansi at the centre; it was merely suggested again and again that the regiments were in touch with each other, probably a handful of sepoys in each forming a committee and corresponding. Nor is there a record of any condemned mutineer trying to save his life by revealing such a conspiracy.

The dates of the risings at Meerut, Cawnpore and Jhansi were separated by weeks; their circumstances and characters were diverse and show no evidence of a general plan, merely of widespread, shared and deeply-felt grievances.

'I consider that the native army mutinied of their own accord,' said Ahsan Ullah Khan, 'and not at the instigation of any chiefs, because in the latter case the mutineers would have either themselves proceeded to join their instigator or caused him to join them.' And Sir John Lawrence agreed with the hakim. 'How is that the people or soldiers did not rise simultaneously in insurrection? I am told that the time fixed for it was anticipated by the Meerut outbreak. But if such was the case, how came it then that the news of that outbreak was not followed by immediate insurrection? It was only when the native troops saw how powerless we were that they resolved to convert what was a mere combination against what they fancied to be a gross oppression into a struggle for empire.' The insurrections came first; the cause to be championed, the rebirth of the Mogul Empire, came later.

Certainly Bahadur Shah was not at the centre of a large-scale plot before the uprising at Meerut. Everything points to his being taken by surprise on 11 May. His immediate instinct was to ask the Meerut sepoys to disperse, and within hours of their entry through the Rajghat Gate he was attempting to contact the British, and sent a messenger to the Lieutenant-Governor at Agra. The reactions of Ahsan Ullah Khan were similar; he thought the rising at Meerut and the occupation of Delhi a 'black thunder-cloud that would soon pass'. He advised the King at first to disown the mutineers. He was early regarded with suspicion by the sepoys in general. On the morning of 16 May, the day on which the women and children were massacred near the pipul tree in the courtyard of the palace, a group of sepoys even accused Ahsan Ullah and Mabub Ali of treachery: the sepoys had, they claimed, intercepted a letter signed by Ahsan Ullah inviting the British into the city on condition that Mirza Jawan Bakht, the King's son by his favourite wife Begum Zinat Mahal, was named as the heir apparent. The letter itself was a forgery – the seal was found to be a crude imitation of the device on Ahsan Ullah's ring. But many of the sepoys even believed that the King was implicated, and there was talk of holding Zinat Mahal as a hostage. Nothing suggests that the King was anxious to lead in a war for the restoration of the glories of the Mogul emperors Akbar and Shahjehan, or to lead the faithful in a jehad. He merely, as the historian Malleson wrote, 'assumed the responsibility of the position which had been forced upon him. It is more than probable that the old man, left to himself, would have shrunk from the position.'

His presence was later demanded by the sepoys as a symbol. And on one occasion at least he employed a 'double'. Maniodin, the inspector of police, recorded that the sepoys, reluctant to attack the ridge, asked for the King's presence in the field. 'This he promised to give. A large force was ordered to assemble in the evening. The King headed the force and passed by the Delhi Gate, and showed himself to the assembled troops. Passing by the Lal Dighi Tank (a reservoir) he went on towards the Lahore Gate. One of the Palace dependents was substituted for the King, who secretly retired to the city by a back way.'

Many of the sepoys of the bahadshi, particularly the Moslems, treated the King with a jocular affability. There were elements of egalitarianism in the Moslem movement. Earlier in the century, in the south, some of the revivalists had even founded Jacobin clubs, and advocated the ending of titles and honorific forms of address. It was perhaps as much this spirit among the Moslem sepoys as the doubts about the King's commitment to their cause that induced them to show the disrespect of which he continually complained.

In his sometimes petulant dotage the King's preoccupations had been his Persian verses, his court bulletin, his favourite wife Zinat Mahal, and the furtherance of the cause of her son Mirza Jawan Bakht. He was himself incapable of taking the lead in a conspiracy. But in the hot days just before the fall of Delhi to the sepoys from Meerut there had been an atmosphere of conspiracy in the courtyards of the Red Fort. Mukundlal, who acted as a secretary to the King, said that the attendants used to sit around the entrance to the royal apartments talking of a revolt in the army and the reward of old retainers: they were talking in this way 'only four days before the outbreak'.

There were rumours of a Russian invasion. There had been much wishful thought, and little accurate information, about the fate of the British forces in the Crimean war. Sir Theophilus Metcalfe was told by a Eurasian official six months before the mutiny began that the King had sent an emissary to Russia. 'I know,' he stated, 'that about five or six weeks before the outbreak it was currently reported in the lines of the sepoys, and much discussed among them, that 100,000 Russians were coming from the north, and that the Company's Government would be destroyed, in fact the idea of Russian invasion was universally prevalent.' On about 7 May the same Eurasian official was advised by an agent of the King to leave the service of the Company and join the King's. 'This hot weather,' he was told, 'you will see the Russians all over the place.'

The hope that the Russians would spring to the aid of the mutineers with a mighty army from the north was over-sanguine, and it appears to have withered away in the hot and claustrophobic days of the siege. Help from the Shah of Persia was less of a mirage. Certainly there was correspondence between him and the Red Fort. Mukundlal is a witness to this. A letter was prepared some months before the outbreak and sent to Persia by the hand of one of the King's armed retainers. Its terms were vague, more a rehearsal of the King's grievances than a request for armed assistance in the event of an uprising. It said that 'the English had made the King a prisoner, and put a stop to all those marks of respect to which, as King, he was entitled, and had suspended the appointment of an heir apparent.' It asked for an exchange of letters and visits.

One Muhammad Darwesh wrote to the Lieutenant-Governor of the North-West Provinces on 24 March informing him of the correspondence between the King of Delhi and the Shah of Persia. Describing himself as 'a mendicant of itinerant habits' he stated that he had learnt 'that two men, with letters from the King of Delhi . . . proceeded about three or four months ago towards Constantinople in company with a caravan going to Mecca.' The messenger later told the King, according to Darwesh, that the Shah had taken Bushire, expelled or murdered all the Christians, and that very soon 'the Persian army [would] advance by the way of Kandahar and Kabul towards Delhi.' Bahadur Shah told his informant that he would be entrusted with further letters, and these were presumably taken to Persia on about 1 April by, we are told, messengers wearing 'the coloured garments of religious mendicants'.

All this, Darwesh implied, was common gossip in the courtyards and alley-ways of the Red Fort: 'the conversation night and day is the early arrival of the Persians. Hassan Askari (the messenger) has, moreover, impressed the King with the belief that he has learned, through a divine revelation, that the dominion of the King of Persia will, to a certainty, extend to Delhi or rather over the whole of Hindustan, and that the splendour of the sovereignty of Delhi will again revive, as the sovereign of Persia will bestow the crown on the King.' Succinctly Ahsan Ullah Khan summed up the rumours of April and early May: 'many chiefs,' he said, 'including Bahadur Shah, were of opinion that if the Emperor of Russia were to aid the Persians the English would be defeated and the Persians would become masters of India.'

All this was borne out, too, by an Englishwoman, Mrs Fleming, who visited the Begum Zinat Mahal at the end of April, only about a fortnight before the outbreak. Jawan Bakht, the son of Zinat Mahal who had been passed over by the British as heir apparent, was present with his wife, and Mrs Fleming had brought her daughter Mrs Scully. During the conversation Mrs Scully turned to her mother and said:

'Do you hear what this young rascal is saying? He is telling me that in a short time he will have all the infidel English under his feet, and after that he will kill the Hindus.' Jawan Bakht told Mrs Fleming that he was joking, and was told that if what he said was true his head would be taken off first. But before Jawan Bakht left what can hardly have been an amicable party he said to Mrs Fleming 'that the Persians were coming to Delhi', and that they should go to him for protection after the armies arrived.

One contemporary thought that the correspondence between the King and the Shah was of little significance, and that was Sir Syed Ahmad, one of the few Indians to write authoritatively about the mutiny from first hand. He was not surprised that Bahadur Shah had sent a firman to the King of Persia. Such was Bahadur Shah's credulity 'that had anybody told him that the King of Genii, in fairyland, owed him fealty, he would unhesitatingly have believed him and have written ten firmans instead of one.' There was no strong evidence, he thought, of a serious plot. 'As between Roman Catholics and Protestants, so between the Mussulman of Persia and Hindustan, cordial cooperation is impossible . . .'

So what was the importance of the proclamations that appeared on the walls of the public buildings in Delhi the day before the rebels arrived through the Rajghat Gate, and were torn down by the order of Simon Fraser? The terms were vague, an appeal to all Moslems to join forces against the British, but making no mention of an alliance between the King of Delhi and the Shah of Persia. Where did they come from? Were they authorized by the Shah? That hardly seems likely, for there was no subsequent attempt by the Persians to aid the Delhi, or any other, mutineers. Perhaps the posting of the proclamations was no more than a hopeful gesture by Moslem patriots, an exercise in propaganda. It certainly proved no agreement between the King and the Shah.

What of the other evidence that the rebellious sepoys in Delhi had originally acted and continued to act throughout the siege in compliance with a plan that had been made before the original outbreak in Meerut, a plan that was to involve the civil population as well as the army? There was the distribution of the chapatis. This phenomenon was first noticed in January. Flat unleavened loaves were given with instructions to make sometimes five, sometimes ten more, and to pass them on as a kind of chain letter. Magistrates closely questioned the recipients, but could find no general agreement about what they were meant to convey. Sir John Malcolm noticed similar portents, if indeed they were portents, half a century earlier in the south, before the mutinies at Vellore. The chapatis may have been a signal to the civil population, or they may have been a charm, or they may have been distributed in obedience to a vow.

One explanation of the distribution – it was far-flung and carried out with an amazing swiftness in many districts – was given by Sitaram in his evidence at the King's trial. The chapatis, he told the court, 'were a jadoo or charm' made by direction of the Nana Sahib, who 'took the reed of the lotus, or rumul, called mukhana, and made an idol of it. He then reduced the idol to very small pills, and having made an immense number of cakes, he put a pellet in each, and as far as the cakes were carried, so far would the people determine to throw off the Company's raj.'

The grandees – Bahadur Shah, the Nana Sahib, the Rani of Jhansi, the dispossessed King of Oudh now in disgruntled exile at Garden Reach near Calcutta – all had ambitions to satisfy or grievances to be redressed. There was one who played his part in the early stages of revolt who appears to have had neither ambition nor grievance. Malleson described him as one who 'had not stained his sword by assassination . . . had connived at no murders,' who had 'fought manfully, honourably and stubbornly in the field against the strangers who had seized his country.'

This was the Maulvi Ahmadulla, a native of Arcot in the south. His origins are obscure; he was possibly associated with the Moslem revival movement of the south, which was a movement at once ascetic, nationalist and egalitarian. He was almost certainly the originator of placards that appeared in Madras in January 1857 which declared that the British 'had now abandoned all principles of justice and were bent on appropriating the possessions of the Mahommedans, and that there was but one way of resisting their encroachments – a holy war.' Shortly after this he began a tour of northern India. In mid-January he was in Lucknow with a large number of retainers, preaching a jehad, distributing proclamations, and 'calling upon the faithful and even the Hindus, to arise, or be ever fallen.' Next month he entered Fyzabad in state, with horses, camels and men under arms. A warrant was issued for his arrest, and the Maulvi was captured after a skirmish in which his followers inflicted losses on the company of infantry who had been sent to capture him. He was confined in the cantonments of Fyzabad, and managed to escape when the sepoys of that place rose to join the mutineers.

The Maulvi was motivated by two things: a burning patriotism, and the notion of the holy war. But the two do not seem to have been mutually exclusive. His appeal was to Hindus no less than to Moslems. It was otherwise in the Mogul capital under siege. There was, in that heavy, laden atmosphere, always the fear of a holy war directed as much against the Hindus as against the feringi. It was the Hindus for the most part who kept their shops shuttered and barred. At times the walls were placarded with proclamations against them. The King – who alone was always aware of the danger of civil war within his own camp – even had to issue orders against the Moslems killing cattle in violation of the religious feelings of the Hindus.

Thus, only days after the fall of the city to the bahadshi a proclamation was issued 'to all Hindus and Mussulmans'. It said that the English had 'entertained evil designs – first to destroy the religion of the whole Hindustani army, and then to make the people by compulsion Christians.' It was claimed that the rebellion had been 'solely on account of our religion', urged those who 'disliked turning Christian to act with one heart', and all Hindus and Mussulmans to unite together. But on 19 May, the green standard of holy war was raised in the Jumma Masjid by the Moslems; this brought remonstrations from the King. On the next day the Maulvi Mohammed Sayyid had an audience of the King. He, according to Jeewan Lall, 'pointed out that the Hindus were leaning towards an alliance with the English and had no sympathy with the Mohammedans, and were already holding themselves apart.' The King described the idea of a holy war as 'extreme folly' and 'quite impossible'.

News of the communal feelings within Delhi reached the forces on the ridge. General Reed wrote to Lawrence on 14 June: 'they are displaying the green flag in the city and bullying the Hindus who are praying for our Government – so says our secret intelligence.' Too easily was Islam associated with patriotism, for the revival of the Mogul empire would be the revival of a Moslem empire. Twenty years after the mutiny an Englishman was told by a Moslem prince that 'what he did not like about the Mutiny was that most of them were Hindus.'

Certainly in general throughout Northern India it was the Moslems who were most active in the mutiny. In Agra among the lawyers it was the Moslems who first deserted the British; and a court official wrote that the Hindus 'exerted themselves to protect the property of their English judges, preserved our houses and moveable property, and did whatever they could to show their loyalty and affection.' At Benares and Jhansi it was much the same. The Moslem leader at Bareilly felt that he had to offer an inducement in his proclamations to win over the Hindus – if they joined the reward of their patriotism would be a prohibition against the killing of cattle.

From June to September the advantage ought to have been with the defenders. Delhi proved impossible to invest. At all times the mutineers had unlimited access to the south and to the east; the attempt of Baird Smith to cut their communications by destroying the bridge of boats was unsuccessful. The city itself was the most defensible in all India: one vast fortress, enclosed by walls and ditch, half-encircled by the unfordable Jumna, dominated by the Selimgarh Fort to the east and the gun-emplacements on the walls to the west. At their fullest strength there were approaching forty thousand sepoys for the defence, who had been trained in the usages of war by some of the ablest officers of the Empire. They did not lack ammunition: the new arsenal outside the walls had fallen into the hands of the mutineers by nightfall on 11 May. They did not lack, after the brigade from Bareilly entered the city, at least one talented commander, Mohamed Bakht Khan.

What the defenders did lack was support, strategic rather than tactical, from other parts of revolutionary India. The British depended on a single and precarious life-line that led from the ridge to the Punjab; they were greatly outnumbered – in all India on the eve of the mutiny there were seven sepoys to every soldier from the Queen's regiments; the loyalty of the sepoys who had originally remained true to their salt was constantly in question; they were operating, especially around Delhi, in districts where the inhabitants were by and large hostile.

Help for the defenders from Persia or Russia was a mirage: Jeewan Lall and Maniodin hardly mention it as a subject of discussion in Delhi once the city had fallen to the bahadshi, and the possibility seems to have been relegated to the world of make-believe. Help could have come from the Nana Sahib, who by July and August controlled most of the Gangetic plain to the east. The best interests of the mutineers would have been served by the severing of the British lines of communication to the north-west, which would have starved the besiegers on the ridge, prevented the arrival of the siege-train and Nicholson's movable column. But the Nana Sahib never attempted this. He was jealous of the claims of Bahadur Shah, uninterested in the fate of those defending the Mogul capital, and concerned only with furthering his ambitions in the area of Cawnpore. One who might have seen the strategic implications of the British position outside Delhi was the Maulvi, but he was engaged at Lucknow.

The tiny force on the ridge – apart from their superiority in organization and discipline – had two advantages: their line of communication was to a certain extent protected by the Cis-Sutlej chiefs in the north-west and they had the support of the Sikhs – an irony this, as the Sikhs were the most recently conquered after the bloody wars of the 1840s.

By mid-September these advantages told. The morale of the defenders and the civil population of Delhi was low. Jeewan Lall reported that when the first salvoes of the artillery barrage crashed against the curtain of wall most of the inhabitants would have fled the city if the authorities had not restrained them. There were continual crises among the sepoys of the bahadshi over pay and provisions. There were quarrels among the shahzadas which the King was incapable of resolving. Shopkeepers were clinging to their wares and the rich to their treasure. Relations between Moslem and Hindu had been strained. The Nana Sahib had other interests than the defence of the strategic pivot of northern India.

But in spite of all this, on the eve of the assault morale among the sepoys of the bahadshi rose, for all that so many of the citizens contemplated flight. Great casualties had been sustained among the gunners, but infantry had enthusiastically filled the vacant places at the guns on the walls. The King held a final audience at the Diwan-i-Khas, and Bakht Khan, who was to disappear after the city was retaken, showed some of the personal qualities of a Nelson or a Rommel. With remarkable ingenuity and courage the breaches in the curtain of wall near the Moree Bastion were filled in, when, as yet unknown to the defenders, the assaulting columns were being formed up near the Flagstaff Tower on the ridge. The King, the princes and the general had realized that the heavy bombardment of the past few days was the prelude to an assault by escalade, and key places in the city as well as the walls were heavily defended – the Queen's Gardens, the Jumma Masjid and the Red Fort itself. The narrow alley-ways of the western part of the city, with their high-walled houses and narrow windows, provided a maze of death-traps for assaulting troops; a terrible toll was to be taken by the snipers of the bahadshi.

It has been claimed by Indians as well as English that the main desire of the mutinous sepoys was loot – that they were, whether in the King's army or the Company's, mercenaries; that they were, as Professor Majumdar pointed out, 'very different from the idealized picture of brave patriots fighting for their country's freedom which has been drawn by misplaced sentiments of a later age.' But the greed for loot, the quarrels over pay, the distrust of Hindu for Moslem disappeared in the dawn when the sepoys on the walls saw the men of the 60th Rifles break cover in the scrub, and, in a skirmishing formation, provide themselves the signal for assault.

Chapter Six

ASSAULT

'You are determined that I shall not have a moment's sleep tonight.'

For a week the artillery pounded at the curtain of wall by the Moree Bastion, the Water Bastion and the Kashmir Gate. Then, on the eve of assault, batteries were constructed close to the walls, in front of Metcalfe's house and Ludlow Castle. Coolies working under Major Brind at Battery No. 1 which was bombarding the curtain of wall close to the Moree Bastion showed a remarkable steadiness under fire. Julius Medley of the Engineers watched them at work. 'As man after man was knocked over,' he wrote, 'they would stop a moment, weep a little over their fallen friend, prop his body in a row along with the rest, and then work on as before.' The battery's commander, we are told by one who served with him through the siege, was indefatigable: 'We talk about Victoria Crosses – Brind is a man who should be covered with them from head to foot.' It was indeed said of him that he never slept, and when the men in the battery were exhausted, would take a musket himself, order them to rest and announce 'Your commandant will defend the battery.' And Baird Smith said of him that 'his restless bravery never halted'. The function of the battery under Major Brind was diversionary: the main attack was to be on the extreme left, and the pounding of the Moree Bastion was to draw the enemy's attention. This had been achieved by the 10th when there was an accident – piles of brushwood surrounding it were ignited by sparks from the portfires and the whole battery went up in flames.

The main bombardment then fell to the gunners of Battery No. 2, the most forward and the largest of the artillery positions. It was sited in front of Ludlow Castle within six hundred yards of the walls and contained five howitzers, nine 24-pounder guns and two 18-pounders. The gunners throughout the operation were under continual musket fire from the walls.

The plan of the assault, largely the work of Colonel Baird Smith, was simple but ambitious. It had proved over the months impossible to invest Delhi, that is to surround it with troops and to cut off access to the mutineers. From May to December the mutineers had control of the eastern and southern entries, through the Ajmir Gate, the Calcutta Gate and the bridge of boats. In fact it often appeared that the British forces, not those in the city, were the besieged, and this Barnard had told the Governor-General. The city was to be taken by escalade, after as wide a breach as possible had been made near the Kashmir Gate. The preparations for this were tasks for the sappers: ladders had to be made high enough to reach the parapet on the top of the walls; fascines, large bundles of brushwood, had to be tied to be thrown into the ditch in front of the Kashmir Gate to provide a foothold for the scaling ladders; gabions, cylinders filled with brushwood and rubble to break the impact of bursting shells, had to be constructed and positioned.

Three simultaneous entries were to be made: one at the Water Bastion, one at the bastion near the Kashmir Gate, and one at the Gate itself. Meanwhile a fourth column was to attack the Kishenganj suburb, still held in force by the mutineers, and a fifth column was to be held in reserve. During the assault the camp and the position on the ridge were to be defended mainly by the convalescent.

Overall command of the action was Nicholson's, who also was to command the first column. This, which was to scale the walls by the Kashmir bastion, was composed of all who were fit in the 75th Queen's regiment (about three hundred men), the 1st Bengal Fusiliers and the 2nd Punjab Infantry – a force in all of about a thousand. Nicholson had suggested that engineer officers should accompany each assaulting column, and so young Julius Medley and two other subalterns were attached.

The second column, under Brigadier Jones, was to assault the Water Bastion. It was slightly smaller than Nicholson's – about eight hundred and fifty men from the 8th Queen's regiment, the 2nd Queen's Fusiliers and the 4th Sikh Infantry. Wilberforce Greathed accompanied it as engineer officer. The third column, commanded by Colonel Campbell of the 52nd Light Infantry, was composed of two hundred of Campbell's own regiment, as well as a large force of Punjabi infantry under John Nicholson's brother Charles, and the Kumaon battalion. These three columns were to be launched against the walls.

A fourth column, under Major Charles Reid, was first to capture the suburbs to the south of the British position, and then to enter the city at the Kabul Gate, below Colonel Campbell's position. Reid had eight hundred and sixty men, from his own Sirmoor battalion, from Daly's Guides, some Dograhs and the infantry sent by the Maharajah of Kashmir. A fifth column, with thirteen hundred men and larger than the rest, composed of the 61st Queen's regiment, a wing of the 60th Rifles (who were first to cover the main assault), and Wilde's Rifles, who had only just joined the camp behind the ridge, was to be held in reserve.

The attacking force, including those of the fifth column held in reserve, was only about four thousand men, and the defenders were reliably estimated at ten times that number. It was not, however, their numerical superiority but their superiority in position and fire power that had for so long daunted Wilson, and before him Barnard and Reed. The walls were surmounted by a parapet eight feet high and three feet thick with embrasures for musket fire; there were the gun emplacements at the bastions, with from nine to twelve guns each, and the guns at the Selimgarh fortress at the east of the city had Metcalfe's house within their range. Whatever the attacking force attempted it would be under continual fire from muskets, mortars and field artillery. There was a slender consolation: it had been noticed through the siege that many of the trained gunners among the mutineers had been killed and that their places on the bastions had been taken by infantry.

Once entry had been effected through the Kashmir Gate, the Kabul Gate and the Water Bastion, and the attackers were in the maze of streets behind the walls, none would be able to tell what defences inside the city the mutineers might have constructed. Even Hodson's spies had not been able to produce detailed plans; and Hodson himself was perhaps over-sanguine – 'there is at present nothing to lead one to suppose that the enemy have any intention of fighting it out in the city, after we have entered the breach,' he wrote; 'all, I fancy, who can will be off as soon as we are within the walls.' This was wishful thinking. Whole columns might be raked by musket fire. A successful assault might not mean a final victory.

In those last few hectic days before the assault, when the gunners and sappers in the three forward batteries were working under a hail of musket fire and the crashing of mortars, when Alexander Taylor was carrying out his reconnaissance expeditions sometimes within fifty yards of enemy snipers, when Baird Smith, doped with brandy and opium to deaden the pain from his suppurating ankle, was tirelessly supervising, inspecting and encouraging – the commander of the Delhi Field Force scattered his confetti of lugubrious memoranda. Hodson was fuming about him – 'the present state of things is terrible . . . no head, no brains, no decision.' At about the time that the siege-train had arrived Baird Smith and Nicholson noticed that the General seemed as if his nerve would crack. Earlier he had opposed an assault altogether; now he was angry that there were delays in some of the batteries. He was particularly incensed at the accident in Battery No. 1. He wrote sharply to the Chief Engineer that he considered that the two days' barrage from that battery had been useless, and that 'a large number of artillery men and a large quantity of ammunition (had) been needlessly expended.' Angrily Baird Smith tossed back the ball to his commander: the loss of the battery was serious, 'but trifling in comparison with that which must have resulted from General Wilson's plan, with the small help for working parties and manning batteries!'

There had been, thought Wilson, 'a great and useless delay' caused by 'the engineers' miscalculation and want of arrangement'. It was all most unjust. Then on the eve of the assault the climax came. Wilson told Baird Smith that he was to act now through the Assistant Adjutant-General and not through the commander of the Delhi Field Force. Wilson washed his hands of the arrangements, and General and Chief Engineer would no longer deal directly with each other.

But from the 11th onwards the strictures of Wilson were proved to be unjustified. New batteries had been constructed, one only a hundred and eighty yards from the Moree Bastion, and the barrage that had begun on the 7th was increased. By the end of that day the rebels' guns at the Kashmir Bastion had been silenced, parts of the wall were in fragments, the guns at the Water Bastion had been overturned and a wide breach had been made. There were by now fifty guns and mortars blazing away at the doomed city. 'The din and roar were deafening,' wrote Charles Griffiths; 'day and night salvoes of artillery were heard, roll following roll in endless succession, and striking terror in the hearts of those who felt that the day of retribution was at hand.'

The enemy were answering this bombardment with one of their own. They had field guns in the open spaces in front of the walls, and stuck well to them, and they also held the suburb of Kishenganj from which the British right flank could be harassed and the village of Sabsi Mandi and Hindu Rao's house shelled. During the bombardment on the 11th nearly three hundred and fifty men of Wilson's force were killed. One of the mutineers' guns, a 3-pounder, was well sited through a hole in the curtain of wall and did much damage to Battery

No. 2, in spite of all efforts to silence it. An officer looked over the defences of Battery No. 2 to observe the fire; his head was taken off by a ball from the gun in the hole in the wall, and his trunk fell back among the men at the guns.

The mutineers were acting with great courage. Not only were their gunners keeping up a continual answering barrage, but on the 12th cavalry and infantry made sorties from the Lahore Gate and the Ajmir Gate, and cavalry mounted an unsuccessful attack on the right rear of the camp from Kishenganj, an attack that was thrown off by the Guides and the Punjabis. But in the city itself, wrote the interpreter Jeewan Lall, there were signs of panic. 'The whole city would have been deserted by man, woman and child,' he wrote, 'if the city guards had only permitted them to leave.'

Then, after six days of almost unceasing barrage, when each night rockets had lit up the sky like a fireworks display, came the night of the 13th. At 10 o'clock Julius Medley with a party of half a dozen riflemen from the 60th was in a position far forward of Metcalfe's house and within only a few hundred yards of the walls. He was waiting to make a final reconnaissance to examine the size of the breach in the walls near the Kashmir Gate. With his tiny escort he crawled towards the ditch, sometimes with enemy skirmishers only thirty yards away. Medley dropped into the ditch in front of the crumbling walls and was being passed a light bamboo scaling ladder so that he could climb up to examine the damage to the enemy guns, when he slipped and the sentries heard the rustle of brushwood. Medley and his escort threw themselves on their faces as a rocket from the walls arc-ed into the sky, and, amid a hissing of bullets, they scrambled to safety through the scrub at the top of the escarpment.

Medley reported the state of the breach to Baird Smith. It was this that determined the hour of assault.

But even at this, the eleventh hour, there was obstruction from the commander. Baird Smith of course was no longer dealing directly with Wilson, and the vital information that

Medley had gained in so courageous a reconnaissance was passed to Wilson through the Assistant Adjutant-General. Carping and unjust criticism of the sappers came back to Baird Smith: 'considering that the artillery officers perform ten times the work yours do, I do not think they ought to make the excuse of being tired, to save the lives of their brothers blue. Yours sincerely, A. Wilson.' Alexander Taylor, Baird Smith, Nicholson and the other commanders of the columns were unanimous: the breach had been made, no time should be allowed for the enemy to repair it, no time for him to re-position his own batteries. 'I should say that the assault on the water bastion is *hopeless*,' Wilson was scribbling to Baird Smith an hour after Medley's reconnaissance; 'there is no approach to it apparently. What do *you* propose?' And, he added plaintively, 'You are determined I shall not have a moment's sleep tonight.'

It was not only General Wilson who had not a moment's sleep that night. At midnight Baird Smith went to the General's tent. It was the first time the two men had spoken for several days. Curtly the General was told of the opinion of the engineers, the artillery, the commanders of the columns – that further bombardment would exhaust the gunners in the batteries, that to delay the assault would allow the enemy to reorganize his defences, even to repair the breaches in the walls. Wilson at last allowed the order to be given.

Then from the batteries on the ridge, in front of Metcalfe's house and Ludlow Castle the guns ceased firing, and the crashing and smoke of a week-long barrage gave way to an eerie, chilling silence. For six days the nerves of officers and men had grown accustomed to an almost continual deafening roar; now an ominous calm descended on the ridge and the rock and scrub and gullies that lay between the camp and the doomed city. At midnight the hurricane lamps flickered in the mess-tents and the tents of the commanders of the five columns. Maps of oiled paper crackled as they were unfolded. Few in the lines had slept; the men who were to form the columns had retired to their tents clothed and equipped, and the news spread from one little cone of canvas to the next that the walls were to be assaulted as soon as the first streaks of light appeared in the morning sky.

At 3 o'clock, while it was still dark, the men mustered near the Flagstaff Tower. Uniforms were in tatters, boots mildewed by the corroding rains; some of the officers wound puggris round their heads to form a turban as protection against falling masonry; one subaltern borrowed a clean shirt from a companion – and kept it after the assault as a memento of its owner, who was killed; another wrote a letter to his wife, then tucked it into the bands of cloth that he had wound round his head.

In the silent darkness the men were given a double issue of rum, and then heard their orders. They were simple. Any who fell wounded during the assault were to be left where they lay: in the initial minutes every man who could stand would have his task, and none could be spared as stretcher-bearers. There was to be no quarter given to the mutineers, and no prisoners were to be taken – but no harm was to come to women or children ('No fear, sir!' from the ranks). There was to be no looting: prize agents had been attached to the Field Force and the spoils of war would be distributed after the city had been captured. When these orders had been read by the light of a hurricane lamp, the officers drew their swords and took a solemn oath of compliance. The oath was repeated by the men in the ranks.

Then in the silence under the stars a venerable figure approached the ranks of No. 1 Column. It was the white-bearded Father Bertrand, a French Catholic missionary who had helped Rotton in the endless visits to the field hospitals during the past three months: 'a pattern Roman Catholic priest,' the chaplain later wrote of him 'who lived as sparingly as a hermit, while he worked as hard as an English dray-horse.' Father Bertrand asked if he might address the men of the column, and while the men in the ranks bowed their heads he prayed, his vestments fluttering in the night breeze, for mercy on the souls of those hundreds certain to be killed in the scrub, in the ditches and on the walls.

At about 3.30 a.m. No. 1 Column – Nicholson in front with a small detachment from the 60th Rifles – moved off across the scrub and the stones towards the centre of the position from which the assault was to be made, Colonel Campbell's column to his left and Brigadier Jones' to his right. Before the sun rose the dispositions were complete, and they had been made without the enemy's knowledge. At about 4 o'clock Nicholson went from column to column, asking in a calm voice for assurance from the leaders that the men were in position.

At first light, when the signal to advance should have been given to Columns No. 1 and No. 2, there was an agonizing delay. Young Ensign Wilberforce was with the columns. 'Something had gone wrong,' he wrote later, 'no one of us knew exactly what it was, but we stopped for an hour and a half, losing the precious darkness, and watching the daylight creep up into the sky.' Many of those who should have been in the field hospitals had surreptitiously joined the assaulting columns; at this point these, weakened by fever and dysentery, fell out. The delay was soon explained; it was found that the enemy had already made extensive repairs to the breaches since Medley's reconnaissance only six hours before, and that sandbags and fascines had been piled in the gaping holes in the masonry. The men of the attacking columns were forced to lie on their faces, still and tense, within so short a distance from the walls, while artillery and mortars again crashed forth against the hastily improvised defences of the mutineers. Then, once again, the din ceased and the smoke drifted away into the dawn air.

Nicholson went calmly over to Brigadier Jones and put his arm round his shoulder. 'Is everything ready?' he asked in a deep calm voice. The signal to advance, he told the Brigadier, would be a dash made by the men of the 60th who were in front of Column No. 1.

Meanwhile Wilson, Baird Smith and the staff had made their headquarters at the top of Ludlow Castle where they could watch the action of the first three columns. Charles Griffiths was with the reserve column, and from the rising ground at the foot of the ridge he saw it all. The first to move were the riflemen of the 60th. Griffiths heard their cheer, saw them make for the walls in a skirmishing formation and heard the rattle of musketry from the mutineers. Then, seconds later, the two thousand men of the first two columns broke cover and rushed the ditch and the two breaches in the walls, the detachments of engineers carrying ladders in the front.

'The ramparts and walls and also the top of the breaches were alive with men,' Griffiths wrote, 'who poured in a galling fire on our troops.' The casualties were heaviest when the scaling ladders were being put up under a hail of bullets and loose masonry thrown from the parapets. The ladders were not high enough, and so the sappers piled up the corpses of the fallen as a pedestal. For Column No. 1 the assault was quick and successful. Nicholson himself, accompanied by Lang, one of the young engineer officers attached to his column, found he needed no ladder and scrambled up the stones and jagged, fallen masonry through the breach at the Kashmir Bastion. 'The bullets seemed to pass over us like a hissing sheet of hail,' wrote Lang, 'and the noise of the cheering was so great that I could hardly make myself heard.'

Nicholson was one of the first through the walls in No. 1 Column. Almost simultaneously came Julius Medley with the men of the 75th, scrambling down the ramps and into the city near the Main Guard, within yards of the spot where Colonel Ripley had been hacked to death with bayonets four months before, and from which Le Bas, Edward Vibart and Mrs Forster had tried to make their escape to the Flagstaff Tower. As soon as the column had rushed the breaches and scaled the walls, losing all but ten of their thirty-nine ladder men, the mutineers began to fall back into the narrow lanes of the western quarter of the city. To Wilberforce Greathed it was a beautiful sight: 'We could see the two columns on our right climbing up the breach like a swarm of bees, or rather like the horses of the sun all abreast, then like hounds topping the fence into a gorse cover they disappeared into the town; it was really a glorious thing to see . . .'

The third column was to enter by the Kashmir Gate itself, which had first to be blown. This was to be done by two engineer subalterns, Duncan Home and Philip Salkeld, accompanied by three British sergeants, four native sappers, a havildar and a bugler to give the signal when the great wooden gate flanked and topped by masonry had been blown in. Each man carrying a 25 lb. bag of explosive, the little group dashed through the boulders and scrub towards the ditch in front of the gate, the mutineers too astonished to do anything but fire a few random shots which went wide of their mark. Too late, when Home, Salkeld and their party had reached the wrecked timber drawbridge, the mutineers realized their mission and poured fire on them from the open wicket in the main gate.

One of the sappers and a sergeant were killed as they were laying the powder bags, and the havildar was severely wounded. But Salkeld and one of the sergeants managed to get the powder bags so close to the wall that they were partially hidden from the mutineers at the loop-holes and the wicket. Just as he was about to pass the lighted fuse, however, a bullet hit Salkeld in the thigh. He reeled, dazed and in agony, and pressed the fuse into the hands of Sergeant Burgess before toppling back into the ditch. The fuse, however, had gone out and, as the third sergeant, Smith, was lighting a lucifer for him, a bullet ripped into Sergeant Burgess and he, too, fell backwards into the ditch. Sergeant Smith was now alone with the powder bags at the foot of the wall below the Kashmir Gate. He lit the fuse, set it to the bags of powder, and just had time to jump clear to safety as the timber and masonry went up into a cloud of smoke. When the smoke drifted away and the dust settled Sergeant Smith saw that Salkeld and Burgess were still alive covered in rubble at the bottom of the ditch. He and the bugler Hawthorne dragged them to safety under what was left of the drawbridge. The bugler was ordered to sound the signal to advance; he had to sound it three times to make himself heard above the noise of the muskets and the crashing of falling stones.

The signal was heard, and No. 3 Column entered the city through the shattered gate with little opposition, followed by No. 5 Column which until then had been held in reserve. The explosion, according to Julius Medley, had brought down only half of the gate, and the passage beyond it was 'choked with rubbish'. Soon the gateway was thronged with the gunners and their ammunition going into the city, and the wounded on doolies (stretchers) being taken out and eventually back to the ridge. Medley was there within minutes of the blowing of the gate and described the wounded: 'Most of the sufferers quiet and insensible from loss of blood, others groaning in agony; and some came staggering up, supported by their comrades, the leaden hue of the countenance, and fixed, glazed expression of the eye, telling that they were struck in a vital part, and had but a short time to live.' Within an hour of the first charge of the men of the 60th four of the columns were in the city being re-formed under Nicholson at the Main Guard.

By midday the assault on the walls had been brilliant, successful and swift. It was otherwise with Major Reid's column. His orders had been to clear the Kishenganj suburb and enter Delhi by the western gate, his plan had been to capture a high point in the suburb, the Idgah, before dawn, and then to march the main body of the column from its forming-up place outside the Sabsi Mandi picket, capture the mutineers' guns and turn them on the city. Then he was to advance along a dry ditch to the Kabul Gate, south of the points of entry of the other columns, and join forces with Nicholson.

But two things thwarted his plans. The first was the failure of his guns to arrive at the start. After consideration, however, he decided to advance as planned on the suburb, without the guns, and trusting that a detachment of Kashmiris had secured the Idgah. The second was a premature attack made by Reid's Kashmiris: seeing mutineers streaming out of the suburb and from the Kabul Gate they were unable to hold their fire. When Reid reached the dry ditch along which he and his eight hundred and fifty men were to make their way to the Kabul Gate he found it was swarming with mutineers. He exposed himself to make a quick reconnaissance and was hit and wounded.

Confusion followed. Some officers, seeing the strength of the mutineers and realizing that it was now impossible to reach the Kabul Gate by way of the dry ditch, ordered their men to draw back. The Kashmiris were charged by a large force of mutineers and retreated headlong towards Sabsi Mandi. A party of the 60th who had not realized that Reid was wounded and out of the action were given conflicting orders. The whole force, in disarray, was being pushed back towards the ridge. The reverse was serious: for a time it seemed to Chamberlain, from his vantage point at the top of Hindu Rao's house, as if the mutineers would annihilate Reid's column, capture the ill-defended British camp, and then be able to make their way back into the city. He and Captain Daly, both too ill to walk or ride, were carried in doolies to the scene of the rout and were able to check it and hold the position in front of the village of Sabsi Mandi.

The failure of Reid's column had its effect inside the city. After assembling at the Main Guard the four columns were rearranged by Nicholson into two. Columns Nos. 1 and 2 joined forces and moved to their right to clear the walls in the direction of the Lahore and Kabul Gates, where they should have been joined by Reid and his men. The other two columns penetrated the city – No. 5 towards the Jumma Masjid which was its objective, Colonel Campbell's towards the College Gardens.

During the assault casualties had been high; but the enemy at least had always been visible, firing from the parapet or hurling masonry at the men climbing the ladders. There had been no time for thought. Fear and anxiety were driven out of

Above The courtyard of the palace in Delhi and scene of the massacre of Christians on 16 May.
Below The terrain between the ridge and the walls of Delhi.

Above The Sabsi Mandi picket on the ridge.
Below The Kashmir Gate immediately after the assault.

the men by the urgency of what they were doing; their officers were among them, on ladders, in the rubble, on top of the walls. They were buoyed up by their own cheering, the closeness of the formations, and, once the breaches had been rushed and secured, by their evident success. It was otherwise once the columns were inside the city. Here the streets and lanes were narrow, the houses on either side of them high and their windows small. 'From every window and door,' wrote Charles Griffiths who was making his way with Column No. 5 towards the College Gardens, 'from loopholes in the buildings and from the tops of the houses, a storm of musketry saluted us on every side, while every now and then, when passing the corner of the street, field guns loaded with grape discharged their contents into the Column. Officers and men fell fast . . .'

The soldiers reached and took the College Gardens by midday, bayonetting the rebels and clearing the houses that surrounded the open space. Here the infantry who had made the assault were assisted by cavalry. Hodson was himself among them, and an officer writing home to his wife described him in this action, sitting on his horse 'like a man carved in stone, and as calm and apparently unconcerned as the sentries of the Horse Guards; it was only by his eyes and ready hands that one could tell the danger he was in, with balls flying amongst us as thick as hail.'

Colonel Campbell's column was not so successful. They had no powder with which to blow the gates of the Jumma Masjid and were forced to fall back and to occupy themselves clearing the lanes and alley-ways near the Kashmir Gate, having joined forces with Column No. 5. 'Isolated groups of men, European and native,' wrote Griffiths, 'led sometimes by officers but often without any leaders, roamed through the narrow streets, entering houses from which the fire was more than usually severe, and putting to death without mercy all who were found inside.' Often the mutineers would flee from their positions, using a crowd of yelling and screaming women as a cover, knowing that the British troops would not fire on them.

By nightfall important positions on the walls were still untaken. The first two columns had as their objective the Lahore Gate and the position known as the 'Burn Bastion' which was close to it, but the rebels held these in force; field guns and howitzers poured grape and canister into the assaulting columns, and musketry rained on them from the adjoining houses. Many attacks were made, but at last, worn out, the two columns had to retire to the Kabul Gate and the position they already held.

During the day Column No. 3 as well had failed to achieve its objective. They had been able to blow a gate in the Begum Bagh, the Queen's Garden, and advance up the wide, mile-long street of the silversmiths, the Chandni Chouk, that cut the city in two and led from the Lahore Gate and the Jumma Masjid. In the Chandni Chouk they met little opposition, but outside the mosque they were met by a dense crowd which, with suicidal bravery, hurled themselves on the force with tulwars. Colonel Campbell's engineer officers had been killed; he had no powder and no artillery with which to blast his way into the mosque and to hold it. It looked as if the column might be cut off by mutineers in the Chandni Chouk to their rear; and so piling his wounded on to charpoys, beds of string and webbing, and shutters torn down from windows, Colonel Cambell withdrew to join the other columns in the area around the Kashmir Gate.

Earlier in the day Julius Medley had been wounded in the arm, and walked out of the Kashmir Gate to have it attended to by the surgeon on the ridge. As he came through the gate he found two of his servants there to meet him, bringing cold food for his breakfast and several bottles of lemonade. 'I have seldom had a more refreshing drink than that,' he wrote, and he gave one of his bottles to a man who had had his thigh shattered, who thanked him 'with the most eloquent look'.

By the end of the day only one column, the second, had achieved its objective. The others had fallen back on the positions around the Kashmir and Kabul Gates, and there they settled for the night. Fires were lit, tea was brewed, sentries and pickets posted; and then the casualties were reckoned up. The slaughter on the walls and in the ditch had been great; many during the day had simply disappeared – entering houses to flush out mutineers, they had never been seen again; a heavy toll had been taken during the capture of the College Gardens, a heavier one outside the barred gates of the Jumma Masjid.

On the 14th about twelve hundred men had been killed or simply disappeared, about a quarter of the whole assaulting force. The enemy dead were impossible to compute: 'dead bodies lay thick in the streets and open spaces,' wrote one officer, 'and numbers were killed in the houses; but the greater part of those who fell were no doubt carried off by the rebels.' For the first hours in the city many soldiers made no distinction between mutineers and civilian men. 'There is no more terrible sight than a city taken by storm,' wrote the same officer, 'all the pent-up passions of men are here let loose without restraint. Roused to a pitch of fury from long-continued resistance, and eager to take vengeance on the murderers of women and children, the men in their pitiless rage showed no mercy.'

One of those to fall was John Nicholson himself. It had happened in the early evening. Nicholson realized the supreme importance of capturing the Lahore Gate, which controlled the great artery of the city, the Chandni Chouk; and so he himself led a party of the 75th, the 1st Fusiliers and some Sikhs along a narrow lane by the side of the wall which led to the gate. The lane was only ten feet wide, with high buildings on either side from which snipers were picking off the leading groups. Turning a corner in the lane the men – who had fought all day in the ditches, on ladders, on the parapets and in the maze of streets in the city – wavered and hung back. Nicholson was at the time at the rear of the column; immediately he ran to the front and drew his sword. 'I never thought Europeans would quail before heathens,' he shouted. At that moment he staggered and fell; a bullet had ripped into his ribs and grazed his lung. A sergeant pulled him into cover and offered him some brandy from his flask, but Nicholson waved him away, saying that he would not be moved from the spot until the lanes had been cleared. Losing consciousness the General was placed on a doolie and carried out of the city.

During all this Frederick Roberts was at General Wilson's headquarters at Ludlow Castle. Wilson, Roberts noticed, 'was ill and tired out'. All through the latter part of the day he had had discouraging reports. He had heard of the failure of Reid's column to clear the suburbs and of Campbell's to capture the Jumma Masjid. He had heard (which was untrue) that both Hope Grant of the cavalry and Tombs of the horse artillery had been killed. And then he heard that the commander of the assaulting columns had fallen seriously wounded. He was beginning to consider withdrawing completely from the city and re-forming the columns on the ridge.

It was at this point that Wilson sent Roberts into the city to make an appreciation. As he approached the Kashmir Gate Roberts saw a doolie on the ground with no bearers. He dismounted and found to his grief and consternation that the occupant was Nicholson 'with death written on his face . . . He was lying on his back, no wound was visible, and but for the pallor of his face, always colourless, there was no sign of the agony he must have been enduring.' To Roberts it seemed a terrible blow, one that might result in the failure to capture Delhi itself. 'I never felt as I felt then – to lose Nicholson seemed to me at that moment to lose everything.' Roberts discovered that the doolie-bearers had dumped their charge and gone off to plunder, and were at that moment 'busy ransacking the houses and shops in the neighbourhood, and carrying off everything of value they could lay their hands on.' It was with difficulty that he could find four men and a sergeant of the 61st; he took down the sergeant's name, told him who the wounded officer was, and ordered him to be taken to the field hospital. 'That,' wrote Roberts years later, 'was the last I saw of Nicholson.'

At first the surgeons thought he would recover, for the

bullet had not penetrated the lung. But Nicholson himself had no such hope. He told Roberts when he was rescued by him at the gate 'there is no chance for me.' He told the surgeons that 'the chill of death' was on him. In fact he was to linger on for another nine days in great pain. Brigadier Chamberlain was the first officer to see him that night. Nicholson was lying on a charpoy and had been given doses of opium to deaden the pain. He did not tell Nicholson of the poor state of the column and the magnitude of the failure of Reid's force – although he had been dictating a discouraging memorandum to an A.D.C. when he was called – but told him instead that he had impressed upon Wilson the need 'to hold the town until the fall of the last man.' Hope Grant, too, visited Nicholson late that night. He found him motionless, stretched on a charpoy, attended by an Indian servant, and he looked, thought the colonel, like 'a noble oak riven asunder by a thunderbolt'. At first Nicholson could not recognize his visitor, and then, after a long pause, he was able to mumble some words of thanks. Then came his brother Charles, whose shattered arm had been amputated, and he was placed on a stretcher at his side. During that night the General slipped into a coma. The huge bewhiskered Pathan slept in front of the flap of the tent.

Roberts completed his mission in the city and reported back to Archdale Wilson at Ludlow Castle. He was able to tell him that Hope Grant and Tombs were alive, that the College Gardens had been secured, that the area immediately surrounding the Kashmir Gate was occupied and that most of the mutineers had withdrawn to the eastern parts of the city; but all this did not dispel the General's despondency. There was the failure of Reid to clear Kishenganj, of Campbell to occupy the Jumma Masjid and of the first column to capture the gun emplacements at the Burn Bastion and the Lahore Gate. Above all there was the wounding of Nicholson. 'His dejection increased,' wrote Roberts, 'and he became more than ever convinced that his wisest course was to withdraw from the city.' This, Roberts thought, Wilson would have carried out – in spite of the fact that every officer on his staff was for seeing the operation through – if it had not been for Baird Smith to whom Wilson at last turned for advice. 'We *must* hold on,' Baird Smith told him in 'such a determined and uncompromising tone,' wrote Roberts, 'that it put an end to all discussion.'

The day ended with massive casualties, with a small force clinging to the fringes of the city, with a base camp still threatened, and the most determined and inspiring leader lying comatose and mortally wounded in his tent. The field hospitals were full; James Rotton and the surgeon Edward Hare were again at work through the night; the alleys of Delhi were littered with the dead, the flies were clustering. It had been a day of omen: as John Nicholson had shouted to the men on the scaling ladders that morning, it was the third anniversary of the Crimean battle of Alma – a glorious episode in a sometimes far from glorious campaign.

Chapter Seven

CAPTURE

'I suppose my people gave themselves up to the devil.'

At 8.30 in the morning of 15 September young Octavius Anson was sitting in the sun outside the walls of Delhi writing a letter. A swarm of black ants was irritating him. 'We have taken all the wall from the Water Gate to the Lahore; what else I cannot possibly say. Rumour has it that the magazine and treasury at Jumma Masjid are ours.' But rumour was wrong. The men of the columns had, on the day of the assault, merely penetrated the western parts of the city. The great artery of the Chandni Chouk leading to the palace and the Jumma Masjid, the Lahore Gate and the Burn Bastion, the magazine and the Selimgarh Fort were all still in the hands of the mutineers. Wilson's headquarters, first in St John's Church and then in Colonel Skinner's house, were raked by rifle and mortar fire. A temporary field hospital had been established in a house just outside the walls; in one of its outhouses corpses were piled awaiting burial; the floors of the rooms were soaked with blood, and bearers were carting away amputated limbs by the score. James Rotton had been joined by another Anglican chaplain, Ellis, and Father Bertrand by an Italian priest. They supervised the digging of a communal grave. In the assault 66 officers and 1,104 soldiers had been killed – about a quarter of the attacking force.

It was now not only Wilson who was pessimistic about the prospects for completing the capture of the city. Chamberlain dictated his appreciation of the situation to an aide-de-camp.

'Our numbers are frightfully reduced, and we have lost so many senior officers that the men are not under proper control,' it ran. 'If the Hindu Rao picket cannot be moved, I do not think we shall be strong enough to take the city.' Wilson of course wanted to withdraw and re-form his depleted forces on the ridge. A subaltern, Reginald Wilberforce, saw him talking to a group of senior officers on the morning of the 15th outside St James's Church. The General looked worn and distracted, and was tugging at his goatee beard. Impulsively Wilberforce put a glass of brandy in the General's hand: he seemed to need it. Colonel Mackenzie thought the commander was 'worn out with illness and want of rest, and with the strain of long continued anxiety,' and that he 'seemed to be losing heart'. There was still that lugubrious attitude that for weeks had exasperated Nicholson and Baird Smith. 'I have not a Queen's officer under me worth a pin,' Wilson wrote, 'or who can preserve any sort of discipline, except Jones of the 60th Rifles. In fact, the men are so badly officered they will and can do nothing. Altogether our prospects are not good.' His opinion was shared by young Frederick Roberts. 'Such a number of woe-begone I think I never saw before in my life,' he wrote. 'All the old officers completely at their wits' ends.'

But it was not only the officers at the Headquarters who were exhausted, some demoralized and at their wits' ends. A new and unexpected hazard had arisen which seemed at first as if it might put most of the European troops out of action. Great stores of liquor had been discovered and looted. By midday on the 15th many of the men were completely drunk. Some officers thought the liquor had been deliberately left exposed by the retreating sepoys, who knew the proclivities of the British soldiery. 'The men were in a very unruly state,' ran an article in *Blackwood's Magazine*. 'Much brandy, beer and other intoxicating liquors were left so exposed by the enemy, that it would seem that they had almost been left about purposely.'

The officers tried to persuade the men that the drink had been poisoned. 'One old soldier, a thirsty soul, taking up a bottle of brandy, and looking at it, said: "Oh, no sir, the capsule is all right – Enshaw and Co. – no poison that." ' Then orders came from the Field Force Headquarters that the barrels and bottles had to be broken, and the liquor was poured away on the streets of Delhi as it had been, once, in the streets of Mecca. Meanwhile, in that terrible field hospital outside the walls, where the mutilated and the dying were groaning on the blood-soaked charpoys, brandy was in desperately short supply.

On the 16th – although so many of the men were drowsy and sullen from the long debauch – Colonel Deacon of the 61st stormed and took the magazine with a party of Punjabis and Baluchis. The casualties were few, but the mutineers made a fierce counter-attack. To throw it off Colonel Deacon's troops climbed into the turrets on the walls of the magazine. 'A soldier of the 61st was shot through the head by my side,' wrote young Edward Thackeray who was with the force; 'the poor fellow lived for about twenty minutes, writhing in agony on the ground.'

Even the good news about the magazine, which he heard at two in the afternoon, could not lift Wilson's spirits. The men had no taste for street-fighting, the bullets from unseen snipers, the unexpected mortars in the narrow lanes, the continual shelling from the area of the palace and the Selimgarh Fort. It was all very different from the sudden, exhilarating assault of two days before. 'It is dreadfully slow work,' Wilson wrote. 'Our force is too weak for this street-fighting, when we have to gain our way inch by inch; and, of the force we have, unfortunately there is a large portion, besides Jummu troops, in whom I place no confidence . . . I find myself getting weaker and weaker every day, mind and body quite worn out. The least exertion knocks me down. I walk with difficulty, and fully expect in a day or two to be laid altogether on my bed . . .'

Two days later Wilberforce Greathed led an unsuccessful attack on the still-untaken Lahore Gate. It was near this place that Nicholson had received the wound that was to prove fatal. Wilson was by now committed to remaining in the city, but Greathed's failure further cast him down, conscious as he was that he had only a little over three thousand infantry inside the walls, and that the enemy probably had ten times that number. 'This is very sad, and to me very disheartening,' he wrote, 'We can, I think, hold our position, but I see no way out at all.' The next day the commander went back to the camp behind the ridge 'to have a good sleep', as Anson said.

For others, meanwhile, the days of capture had not been so wearing. Hervey Greathed, who had been the Civil Commissioner in Meerut, used to go down to Delhi early in the morning, 'to see all that is to be seen' and then return about 1 o'clock to write letters. He dined and slept in the camp.

After the capture of the magazine the front in the city was extended, and advanced positions were taken up on the 17th and 18th. Roberts was in charge of a section of wall between the Kabul and Lahore Gates. He eschewed the tactics of Nicholson, who had tried to approach the Lahore Gate and Burn Bastion along the narrow lanes. He approached the positions house by house – Edward Vibart recorded how this was done. 'The Engineers would first break through the wall of a house, which we at once proceeded to occupy, and then carrying sandbags to the top of the roof, would construct a parapet, from behind which a covering fire was kept up on the next house to be taken.' On the evening of the 19th the Burn Bastion was surprised and taken by a party from the Kabul Gate; and early the next morning the Lahore Gate and the Garstin Bastion fell. It was Roberts who made the reconnaissance that led to the capture of the Lahore Gate. He found a group of grain merchants who led him in secret to a house which overlooked the mutineers' position at the Gate, and there he saw 'the scoundrels of sepoys lolling about and loading a couple of guns, as if they were going to remain masters of Delhi for ever.' From then on the Chandni Chouk was in the grasp of the British troops, and this led to the great prizes, the Selimgarh Fort, the mosque and the palace itself.

The artillery were making great swathes in the city.

Octavius Anson of the 9th Lancers watched it all. On the 17th the general was ' . . . employing our Artillery to knock down the walls and houses of the town and make thereby paths to the points we want to attack, namely the Jumma Masjid, and the Lahore Gate, the Palace and the Selimgarh. It will, I dare say, take three or four days more to drive the enemy out of the city.'

Meanwhile, a stream of refugees was leaving by the gates, deserting the bazaars and shops and houses. It was policy to let the old, and women and children leave, and many sepoys tried to escape in disguise. Soldiers at the gates would lift a veil to find, not a damsel but a moustachioed mutineer: for these there was no quarter and many were shot out of hand.

Some indulged in an orgy of slaughter: young Wigram Clifford, for instance. It was his sister who had been killed when Captain Douglas's quarters were broken into on 11 May, and Clifford wrongly believed that she had first been raped. After hearing the news he had left his civil appointment at Gurgaon and attached himself to the Field Force, volunteering for every expedition against the mutineers that he could. Charles Griffiths met him in the city. 'He shook my hand, saying that he had put to death all that he had come across, not excepting women and children, and from his excited manner and the appearance of his dress – which was covered with blood-stains – I quite believe he told me the truth.'

With so much of the city in a shambles and deserted, the looting began. It had started with the raids by the soldiers on the liquor stores on the 15th. Through the next few days it spread to the empty bazaars and the shops in the street of the silversmiths. Both officers and men were anxious to be ahead of the prize agents. Charles Griffiths and Edward Vibart volunteered to supervise and to prevent the worst excesses. They found more than a dozen crates of treasure in a wall in a shop in the Chandni Chouk. They handed it over, but were allowed first to make a generous selection for themselves.

Looters would examine the books in a house to find out whether the occupants had been Moslem or Hindu. Hindus tended to hide their treasures in holes in the wall, Moslems under the floor. Water was poured on the floors, and the spot where it dried quickest often indicated that something had been buried.

Even young Octavius Anson, a moral and scrupulous officer, helped himself. 'I went nearly through the palace this morning,' he wrote to his wife after the city had been taken, 'and picked up a small drawer full of playthings for the children, things that I might innocently take away as a kind of memorial of Delhi. Amongst them is a mother-o'-pearl lid of a box with a Persian inscription upon it which might do for you to wind a ball of thread on.' Mrs Anson had her mother-o'-pearl lid and Charles Griffiths his fistful of carbuncles which he had made into rings and brooches for his relations, but these were trifles. Later, wherever the 9th Lancers, the 8th of Foot, the 52nd Light Infantry and the 60th Rifles were stationed, Indian jewellery and ornaments would appear for sale in the shops.

On the 17th, Alexander Taylor was severely wounded in the chest, and was out of action for two days. By the 19th, however, he was taking part in the flanking operation that led to the capture of the Lahore Gate and the Burn Bastion. On the next day the assault was made on the palace and the fort. Roberts was there, and wrote of the courage of the remaining defenders from the bahadshi. One sentry at the palace awaited death at his post. 'In a long passage crowded with Native soldiers,' wrote Sir Evelyn Wood, 'a private, 37th Bengal Infantry, stood motionless at The Ready till the stormers were near, when, levelling his musket, he fired; then, charging, he met his death on the bayonets of the King's Royal Rifles.' It was in this action, too, that young Philip Salkeld was fatally wounded. As he was dying, Wilson's aide-de-camp brought him a piece of red ribbon as pledge of the Victoria Cross. Salkeld came from the impecunious service gentry who had built the Raj – his sister was a governess in a suburban household. 'It will be gratifying to them at home,' he murmured.

At last, on the 20th, the Red Fort fell, and the news of it was taken by a breathless subaltern on a sweating horse to Archdale Wilson. Officers lolled at their ease in the great hall of audience, the Diwan-i-Khas, and the men began chipping away at the mosaic and prising out the stones. Above them was the Persian calligraphy: 'If there be a paradise on earth – it is this, it is this.'

Two subalterns stood on the highest point of the fort, where a Union Jack had caught the breeze and stuck out, they noticed, stiff and square like a piece of cardboard. They saw the terrible evidence of a city taken by storm: masonry in ruins, corpses lying thick in the Chandni Chouk, near the Jumma Masjid, in the Queen's Gardens. Parts of the walls were heaps of rubble. Cats, the only moving creatures, prowled in the deserted lanes and alley-ways. There was a hole like a gigantic wound near the Kashmir Gate and another at the Water Bastion.

As Octavius Anson wandered through the city on the 20th, this is what he saw. 'The Kashmir Gate compound was filled with rezais, lotas and other brass utensils, old clothes and all the native rubbish you can imagine taken by the sentries from those camp-followers who had been enjoying the dangerous pastime of looting.' In the morning he had been over all the city except the eastern side by the Jumna, still, precariously, held by the remnants of the bahadshi. He noted, rightly, that 'by this evening, or tomorrow morning at furthest, the city will be wholly in our hands, and "the Siege of Delhi 1857" will be a thing of the past.'

Colonel Bourchier saw the palace. It had, he thought, 'evidently been hastily abandoned'. The King in fact was already in his last, bizarre retreat among the white domes of Humayun's tomb in the old city four miles south of the walls. 'The apartments inhabited by the royal family,' wrote Bourchier, 'combined a most incongruous array of tawdry splendour with the most abject poverty and filth.' He saw Captain Douglas' quarters, the scene of one of the first of the murders. They were 'denuded of every trace of the unfortunate party which had inhabited its walls . . .' Bourchier then went down the length of the Chandni Chouk and saw the houses near the Kashmir Gate. They were 'a mass of ruins, the walls near the breaches were cracked in every direction, while the church was completely riddled by shot and shell . . . In the Water Bastion the destruction was still more striking. Huge siege-guns with their carriages lay about seemingly like playthings in a child's nursery.'

At dawn on the 21st a salute was fired from the fortress of Selimgarh; in high spirits Alexander Taylor rode his horse up the steps of the grandest mosque in the east, while James Rotton prepared to preach at a service of thanksgiving in the hall of public audience of the last of the Moguls.

While the five columns were making their slow and steady progress towards the final goal, the eastern quarters of Delhi with the palace and the forts, Nicholson was lying in his tent, sometimes conscious and sometimes not, for he was taking a long time to die. Every few hours news was brought to him. On the 15th he heard of the failure of Major Reid's column and the reverses in the Chandni Chouk and at the Jumma Masjid. He did not seem concerned with anything except the progress of the attacking force, and spoke of his own wounds, said one officer, in so detached a way that they might have been those of a stranger. He was appalled when he learnt that once all the columns were bivouacked inside the walls, Wilson was again contemplating withdrawal. Rising on one elbow he hissed at Chamberlain: 'Thank God I have strength left to shoot him if necessary!'

It was not an empty threat, and the Commander of the Field Force, wisely, never visited Nicholson's tent. He could still fire a pistol. Some of his Multani horsemen were chattering outside his tent. He called to them to be quiet. After twenty minutes' silence the noise began again, so Nicholson fired a shot from his pistol through the canvas.

Nicholson was concerned that he had left no will, and he began to dictate letters to Chamberlain. One was to his old friend Herbert Edwardes. 'Tell him I should have been a better man if I had continued to live with him, and our heavy public duties had not prevented my seeing more of him privately. I was always the better for a residence with him and his wife, however short. Give my love to them both.' From 21 September, when it was plain that Nicholson was dying, the messages from friends poured in to the ridge. 'Give John Nicholson our love in time and eternity,' cabled Herbert Edwardes; and he invited him to ponder Acts XVI.31 and Romans X.9. Others too were concerned with the state of Nicholson's soul, for he had seemed to lack that implicit faith in a literal interpretation of the Bible that sustained Edwardes, Lawrence and Montgomery. 'Give my love to Nicholson and say how deeply we shall deplore his fall,' ran the message from John Lawrence. 'He is a noble fellow. Tell him to think of his Saviour and pray for His aid which alone can save him.'

Perhaps Nicholson's thoughts in those terrible days and nights were not on his Saviour. They were certainly with his friends and his soldiers, and many felt that his great spirit was willing them to victory. 'My desire,' he said, 'was that Delhi should be taken before I died and it has been granted . . .' On the evening of the 23rd he was talking slowly and very calmly to Neville Chamberlain. 'Remember to tell them that Alex Taylor took Delhi,' he said. Then he turned over on his side, so that Chamberlain thought he had fallen asleep. It was 9.30 in the evening and the General was dead.

They buried him in the little cemetery outside the Kashmir Gate on the morning of the 24th. One British regiment deliberately defied their colonel's order to remain on parade and, instead, attended the funeral. It was a simple affair – the body on a gun-carriage; no salute was fired. The Multani horsemen were there. They had a saying that a man who wept deserved to be beaten by women, but as the earth smacked against the lid of the coffin, they threw themselves on the ground crying uncontrollably. After the burial the Multani horsemen refused to take orders from another commander or to accept any pay. They had come to the detested plains for two reasons, they said: for loot and because 'Nikkul Seyn' had ordered it. So they gathered up their spoils of war and departed for the hills.

On the night of the 19–20 September, when the Burn Bastion fell and the British forces were consolidating their position in the Chandni Chouk, Bakht Khan came to his King and suggested that they both leave the city with as large a force as possible from the bahadshi, and prepare to carry on the rebeliion from another base, perhaps joining up with the mutineers from Lucknow. But the King had another visitor, the degenerate and treacherous Ilahi Bakhsh Mirza who advised that he separate from Bakht Khan and with an escort of retainers from the palace make for the maze of domes four miles to the south of the city, the Emperor Humayun's tomb, and from there try to make terms with the British. The King's only chance, said Ilahi Bakhsh, was to plead that he had been persuaded against his will to head the insurrection. So Mohammed Bakht Khan left the city to continue the struggle: he was never taken. The King, with the shahzadas and a motley crew of about a thousand, some soldiers, some the scum of the palace, left to make his last, bloodless, stand at Humayun's tomb.

Ilahi Bakhsh Mirza then contacted Hodson's chief spy, the one-eyed Rajab Ali. Hodson approached Archdale Wilson for permission to lead an expedition to the tomb and take the King, and was empowered by the commander to offer the King a guarantee that his life would not be taken. So on the 21st Hodson set off with a party of fifty cavalry. There were more than a thousand with Bahadur Shah, many hundreds of them armed: there were look-outs posted on the domes, pickets at the approaches to the maze of buildings. It was Hodson's supreme moment. 'Daring, courting danger, reckless and unscrupulous, he was a condottiere of the hills,' Sir John Kaye wrote of him, 'a free-lance of the Middle Ages. He joyed in the life of camps, and revelled in the clang of arms. His music was the call of the trumpet, the battlefield his ballroom. He would have been at home in the camp of Wallenstein, at the sack of Magdeburg.' All that was needed was a commanding presence and an icy courage as he and his small force entered the death-trap, and then not one of the rabble would raise his rifle against him – not one did.

A message was sent in to the King asking for his surrender. For three hours in the heat of the middle of the day Hodson sat in his saddle and waited for the answer. Then the King intimated that he would parley only with 'Hodson Bahadur'. The guarantee that the King would not be put to death, only that, was given. The King's curtained palanquin came out from the tomb, and the party made its way slowly to the southern gate of the Mogul capital.

At the Delhi Gate some soldiers wanted to give a cheer for Hodson, but were curtly forbidden: the King, they were told, might think it was for himself. Hodson handed the King over to Saunders, the new Civil Commissioner, and reported to Wilson, who told him that he had not expected to see either Hodson or Bahadur Shah again.

The King was placed under guard in a small house in the Red Fort; in the next small room, and within earshot, was Begum Zinat Mahal. He was allowed two annas a day for his food. He had a charpoy, some pillows covered in lace and his hookah. Hope Grant saw him: he was 'short in stature, slight, very fair for a native, and with a high-bred, delicate-looking cast of features.' Edward Vibart saw him too, sitting cross-legged on the bed and gently rocking himself to and fro. He seemed to be reciting verses from the Koran, or perhaps they were of his own composition – Vibart was not sure. He appeared to be 'a small and attenuated old man apparently between eighty and ninety years of age, with a long white beard, and almost totally blind.' He vomited a great deal, for the food was coarse and his digestion had been weak for years.

His conversations with the visitors who came out of curiosity were monitored by his wife, who continually called out to him to be discreet. He was asked by one officer to explain the reason for the atrocities inside the city, the murder of Jennings and Douglas and Miss Clifford, the massacre in the courtyard of the palace. The King could only reply: 'I don't know: I suppose my people gave themselves up to the devil.' The soldiers were discourteous to him in captivity as they had so often been in the days of triumph. His beard was tugged, but Bahadur Shah, now, was past complaining or taking offence. He had outstayed his welcome and he realized it.

On the following day Hodson sought permission to take the princes who had been left at Humayun's tomb. At first Wilson resisted this, but even Nicholson from his death-bed strongly approved the plan, and the commander gave way. At eight in the morning Hodson set off with his second-in-command, Macdowell, and a hundred horsemen – his own troops, 'wild-looking horsemen wearing scarlet turbans and dust-coloured tunics bound with scarlet sashes.' Hodson, tall, spare, riding his horse with a loose rein, was dressed in the same manner.

When the party reached Humayun's tomb Hodson, as he later said, laid his plans 'so as to cut off access to the tomb or escape from it', and Macdowell formed up part of the troop across the road. Then Hodson sent Rajab Ali with 'one of the inferior scions of the royal family', in fact Mirza Ilahi Bakhsh, into the tomb to contact the princes. For half an hour Hodson and Macdowell waited; at times they heard the angry shouts of the Moslems within urging an attack on the infidels who had come from Delhi. Then a messenger came to Hodson to report that the shahzadas were ready to come. An escort of ten was sent. The three princes – Mirza Mogul, a corpulent figure in his mid-thirties, the young and cowardly Mirza Abu Bakr and Mirza Khair Sultan, a grandson of the King – came out in a bullock cart, still in their finery, surrounded by the ten horsemen and followed by a large mob of Moslems. They asked Hodson to guarantee their lives. 'Most certainly not,' he said.

Then something incredible happened. Hodson and Macdowell, heading a force of a hundred and in the face of an enemy many times that number, curtly ordered the Moslems to lay down their arms. And there, in front of the tomb, the arms were piled, five hundred swords and about the same number of rifles. Hodson lingered a while to supervise the collection of arms and to place a guard over it, while the bullock cart with the three princes and an escort moved off along the road towards Delhi, surrounded still by a noisy mob.

Before they had gone more than a few hundred yards Hodson caught up with the party, and sensed that the Moslems might try to rescue the princes. Just short of the Delhi Gate he halted the procession. A crowd was growing and pressing round the cart. Hodson turned to Macdowell. 'What shall we do with them?' he asked. 'I think we had better shoot them here. We shall never get them in.' He placed five troopers in front and five behind the cart. He galloped into the middle of the crowd and reined in his horse. He then delivered a short address: the princes had, he said, been responsible for the murder of women and children, and the government had decreed their punishment. The crowd, as it had been outside Humayun's tomb, was awe-struck, silent and motionless. The princes were told to climb down from the cart and to strip off their clothes down to the loincloths. Hodson took a carbine from one of his troopers and shot each of the three princes dead at point-blank range. Their bodies were taken into the city and displayed outside the Kotwali, the police headquarters.

Hodson claimed that the killing of the princes was done to prevent the crowd from killing him and his own force: 'we should have been most unquestionably sacrificed if I had hesitated for a moment.' And Macdowell supported this, declaring that their own lives 'would not have been worth a moment's purchase'. But the claim is hard to sustain. With only a handful of troops Hodson had been able to disarm more than a thousand at the tomb. It took only ten troopers to hold back the crowd while the princes were stripping, which, as Rice Holmes pointed out, showed that the mob 'at that time had not much stomach for a fight'. Sir Hugh Gough described Hodson's action as 'a false step'; General Reynell Taylor said that he had 'never admitted that their death was necessitated by the danger of rescue'; and Hope Grant commented that 'this sad act was most uncalled for'.

Hodson would never understand why there was such an outcry in some quarters against his action on the 22nd. It all seemed most illogical. 'Strange that some of those who are loudest against me for sparing the King are also crying out at my destroying his sons,' he wrote. 'But, in point of fact, I am quite indifferent to clamour either way.' At the time he seems not to have given it much thought. The mob around his captives greatly outnumbered his own force, and they seemed likely to try to effect a rescue. Seething in his mind was the desire to avenge those murdered in the city, and the blame for this – and not unjustly – he put on the three shahzadas. 'I am too conscious of the rectitude of my own motives to care what the few may say: while my own conscience and the voice of the many pronounce me right . . . These have not been, and are not, times when a man who would save his country dare hesitate as to the personal consequences to himself of what he thinks his duty.' He saw it as an action worthy of self-congratulation. 'In twenty-four hours I disposed of the principal members of the house of Timur the Tartar. I am not cruel, but I confess that I did rejoice in the opportunity of ridding the earth of those ruffians.' The outcry from some mystified and at the same time upset Hodson. 'The only time I ever saw Hodson otherwise than cheery,' wrote General Thomason, 'was one day when I dropped in on him and found him "writing his defence" as he called it, over the matter of the King of Delhi and the execution of the three princes.' He added that at the time he had not heard anyone expressing an opinion about it all other than that the princes had deserved their punishment.

The bodies were laid out in front of the Kotwali in the Chandni Chouk. Here young Edward Thackeray saw them. Lying in their dhotis he thought they 'were dressed like native servants'. Vibart went to the Kotwali and recognized the plump body of Mirza Mogul 'whom I used frequently to meet at picnics and luncheon parties given by the officers of the Delhi garrison, and who often took part with us in rifle competitions and pigeon shooting.' Neither he, nor Thackeray nor Thomason thought that the action of Hodson was anything but justified. Nor did Archdale Wilson. He implied that he did not want to be bothered with any more prisoners when Hodson had asked his permission to lead an expedition to the tomb. The case of the princes differed from the King's. It was common knowledge to the British that they were the evil genii behind the massacres. There was a certain amount of respect for the not un-gallant figure of Bakht Khan; there was contempt mixed with a little pity for Bahadur Shah; but there was nothing but loathing for the degenerates who had presided over and urged the massacre of the women and children beside the pipul tree on 16 May.

The thanksgiving service was conducted in the Diwan-i-Khas, and the text for James Rotton's sermon was: 'What shall I render unto the Lord for all the benefits that He has done unto me?' Nicholson awarded the palm to Alexander Taylor, most of the engineers to Baird Smith, the soldiery to Nicholson himself But the men of simple and rock-like faith – Herbert Edwardes, Montgomery, Lawrence – quite simply gave their thanks to a God mighty in battle. The burials were continuing, but the details who dug the graves and carried the corpses could not keep up with the work. Vultures hovered over the streets littered with the corpses of men and horses. There was a new outbreak of cholera. Over all there was the sickly-sweet smell of death. The men who had fallen were remembered with their officers, officers of the 'unreformed British army' as Sir John Kaye described them, 'men in whom their soldiers had confidence, whose physical energies had not been neutralized by a premature exercise of the powers of the brain.'

After the fall of the city many of the survivors of those who had led the columns were dispersed to other parts of India. The garrison in Delhi was left under the command of Brigadier Neville Chamberlain. He pledged himself to severity with justice. 'I am ready to pass sentence of death against rebels and mutineers against whom any single murder or participation in any act of gross cruelty can be proved, but I would sooner resign my commission than stand a passive spectator of indiscriminate slaughter.' In practice, however, there was little discrimination. The mutineers were rounded up, and the most perfunctory enquiries as to identity were made by hastily set-up courts-martial. Edward Vibart saw it all. '. . . for several weeks subsequent to the capture of the city, wholesale executions of mutineers and other rebels were carried out almost daily. These wretches used to be strung up on a platform in front of the Kotwali, in batches of a dozen at a time . . .'

Hodson left the city, eventually to join the force that attacked the Begum Kothi at Lucknow in March of the following year, as part of the force led by Sir Colin Campbell. He attached himself to a party of Highlanders who had rushed the breaches made in the walls of the great palace. 'Every door and window was barricaded; and bullets flew from every loop-hole,' wrote Rice Holmes. 'One after another the barriers were burst open; the enemy were hunted from court to court and from room to room; and when, after two hours' fighting, the Begum Kothi was won, eight hundred mutineers lay dead in the central court alone.' It was in this action that Hodson, in his thirty-seventh year, fell. He was forcing his way into a small room to flush out some mutineers. Sergeant Forbes-Mitchell of the 93rd was beside him and tried to pull him back. But a shot from a mutineer hit him, and he fell to the ground choking back his blood. Later Hodson's detractors were to claim that he had been in search of loot, but Forbes-Mitchell vehemently denied this. Like Nicholson, he did not die at once, and like Nicholson, he was hit by a chance shot from a mutineer at close range.

All were agreed that Hodson had one virtue in an heroic degree, and that was courage. A friend was asked why Hodson had never been awarded the Victoria Cross, and he replied: 'I suppose he won it every day of his life.' The controversies about his character were to continue from the day of his death onwards. His parson brother tried to vindicate him; he was harshly condemned by the great historians of the sepoy mutiny, by Kaye, Malleson and Rice Holmes. Certainly Hodson was dishonest and untruthful. He was acquitted eventually by the members of the court who enquired into charges of peculation, but, wrote General Crawford Chamberlain at the time of the proceedings, 'the court was very guarded in its language. I don't suppose that Lord D. (Dalhousie) or Sir J. L. (Lawrence) did actually consider 'peculation' proved direct and absolute – but next door to it.' The court stated that throughout its sittings Hodson's evidence had 'abounded in subterfuge' which it 'could not too strongly condemn'. There were other complaints as well – of sharp practice, of abusive language, of an eccentric system of accounting calculated to conceal frauds. Hodson was without fear, but not without reproach.

The conquest had taken six days. On the morning after the assault Colonel Mackenzie wrote that 'the great city, with its intricate network of narrow lanes crookedly piercing through masses of lofty brick-built houses . . . was yet unconquered and defiant.' Everywhere the conquerors went there was evidence of preparation for a fierce resistance once the assaulting columns had scaled the walls. There were piles of sandbags and fascines; there was no shortage of ammunition for rifles, mortars and howitzers. But with the capture of the Lahore Gate and the Burn Bastion the resistance seems to have collapsed. One British officer thought that the mutineers in the last two days or so lacked heart and leadership. This was Captain Daly of the Guides. 'Walking about the streets of

Delhi one could only wonder how we had acquired it,' he wrote. 'The rebels in some places were ready for a stiff resistance. Sandbags in piles, guns loaded to the muzzle and placed in position, all betokened that which they had no leadership or heart to carry out.'

A vast walled city, the most defensible in all India, could not be held by a force of forty thousand against a total British force of thirteen thousand – many of whom throughout were too ill to be in the action at all. At Cawnpore the British, however, could only muster about four hundred, with a small number of loyal sepoys, and many were invalids. The force was besieged in a hastily improvised position with weak entrenchments. Against them were pitted three thousand trained, well armed and well supplied mutineers in a countryside that was favourable to their cause. They could count upon the support of the Nana Sahib, and his powers of leadership and organization were far greater than those of Bahadur Shah. Yet a siege of twenty days failed to give the city to the mutineers. At last, as Professor Majumdar put it, the Nana Sahib 'accomplished by treachery what his valour and heroism failed to achieve.'

It was the same at Arrah. A body of under seventy British and Sikhs held out in a converted billiard room against an attacking force of some four thousand. At Lucknow, as Rice Holmes pointed out, the British had 'less than seventeen hundred soldiers, a large proportion of which were sepoys, some of whom were regarded with suspicion, while others were infirm old men.' The mutineers put in the field against them at least six thousand, trained and well armed. Sir James Outram at Alambagh faced odds of nearly thirty to one; yet he held out from July to September, when he was reinforced by Havelock, and from then on until the final relief in March 1858. These sieges, as an Indian historian puts it, 'show the British valour, heroism, and strategy at their best, and those of the Indians at their worst.'

Was it otherwise at Delhi? There were grave defects in the leadership of the Field Force, but these were concentrated in one man. It is true that Archdale Wilson was debilitated and ill through most of the weeks in which he commanded on the ridge. But Hodson was at times prostrated with dysentery; and so too was Baird Smith, who limped about the camp with a painful suppurating ankle. The real leadership came from the Irregulars, Nicholson, Hodson and Daly; from a few industrious staff officers headed by Chamberlain; and from the engineers whose expertise made the assault possible, headed by Baird Smith and Alexander Taylor. These were men who could improvise; above all they were men who would not be deflected from their purpose once they were inside the walls of the city. Most of them came not from the Queen's regiments but from the humbler ones of the Company. It was this type of officer that had been so greatly lacking in the Crimea two years earlier.

In casualties the siege, assault and capture of Delhi was the most expensive campaign of the sepoy rebellion. Nearly four thousand British troops were killed or wounded. The artillery lost one quarter of its original strength. Disease took its toll: there were few surgeons left by the end and no nurses, and Harriet Tytler, the only woman left on the ridge, was busy among the orderlies in the field hospital. Supplies were poor and the ammunition, particularly for the field guns, was in short supply. The camp at times was a disease-ridden swamp. The flanks of the position were continually exposed to shelling by day and sudden attack by night. There were, it is true, loyal Gurkhas of the Sirmoor Battalion and many loyal Sikhs, but the loyalty of some of the sepoys could not be taken for granted and there were desertions from the sappers to the enemy. The Jhind and Multani horsemen showed a reckless bravery, but the Kashmiris were ill-disciplined and at times unreliable. Above all, by July and August, the force on the ridge could not count on substantial relief, with the mutineers by then controlling so much of the Gangetic plain.

The greatest battle of all was won by Nicholson and Baird Smith, and that was to persuade Wilson to attempt the capture of the city, and having persuaded him, to hold him to that course.

Chapter Eight

REWARDS, RESTORATION AND RETRIBUTION

'No maudlin clemency was to mark the fall of the city'

Richard Baird Smith never properly recovered his health after the siege; nor was he, officially, greatly honoured. He was promoted to Colonel, made a Commander of the Bath and an aide-de-camp to the Queen. But these were honours which would have come to him, perhaps, in the normal course of a worthy career in the Native Engineers. The last years of his life were spent as master of the mint at Calcutta, and he sat on the senate of the university. After the capture of Delhi he made one great contribution to the better government of India, in the report he wrote on the famine of 1861 – there were far-reaching suggestions for the reform of land tenure and the improvement of agriculture and irrigation. At the end of that year, when he was just two weeks short of his forty-third birthday, Baird Smith died on the ship that was to take him back to England.

Archdale Wilson, however, made a quick and complete recovery from the stomach ulcer which had so debilitated him during the weeks when he commanded on the ridge. He was not to die until 1874, at the age of seventy-one. Within weeks of the fall of Delhi he was in command of all of the artillery at Lucknow. Honours came to him in profusion. He was promoted to Lieutenant-General, made Colonel Commandant of the Royal Artillery and a Knight Commander of the Bath. In the new year of 1858 he was created a baronet as Sir Archdale Wilson of Delhi; he received the thanks of both Houses of Parliament and of the Honourable East India Company; he was awarded a pension of £1000 a year.

Others, too, were rewarded. Lord Canning held a series of durbars through 1859. The Maharajahs of Patiala and Jhind were given large grants of land – they had both contributed and kept open routes to the north-west; the Rajah of Kapurthala was given a present of 10,000 rupees, two estates in Oudh and the right to a salute of eleven guns. Sir John Lawrence held a durbar at which the largest property owner of a village was given land and a sword of honour for sheltering and then saving a group of Europeans from the bahadshi. These were the loyal princes: they had helped to protect the Grand Trunk Road and the life-lines to the north-west.

The troops who had taken part in the assault and capture did not fare so well. There was a directive about 'prize', the spoils of war, that was far from generous and in effect handed most of it over to the government of India. Many of the palace treasures, however, found their way to the prize fund, the proceeds, for instance, from the sale of the crown and the crown jewels. The great crystal block and marble platform of the audience hall were sent to England by way of Calcutta. The only certain reward for the forces who had taken part was the grant of an extra six months' 'batta' (special allowances) given by order of the Governor-General.

For others these were the days of retribution. In a circular of March 1858 the Chief Commissioner Sir John Lawrence announced the levying of a compensation tax on all those who had helped the mutineers. In the collection of it, he said, care should be taken that 'plunder and retribution may be in precise proportion.' The object was to provide a fund to compensate for their losses the government and private persons who had remained loyal. The tax fell hardest on Moslems, many of whom paid a 25 per cent levy while the Hindus paid only 10 per cent.

The hangings continued well into 1858. The platform under the beam in front of the Kotwali could accommodate a dozen at a time. By acts of 1857 special commissions had been set up, which could condemn to death without a right of appeal. On 18 November twenty of the poorer relations of the royal house were tried and executed along with chiefs from the surrounding areas who had helped the bahadshi. On 29 May 1858 Hassan Askari, who had held an important position at the court as a soothsayer, was publicly hanged outside the Kotwali before 'a large gathering of the native population, who looked on in silent wonder.' Some were dealt with less officially. Lord Macaulay's nephew George Trevelyan met a corporal who had arrived from England after the capture of the city. The corporal and his companion, Trevelyan was told, overheard 'two Moors talking in a cart mention the word Cawnpore' – so the two soldiers 'polished them both off'.

There were those who wanted a great punishment for the whole city. They felt that it should be razed to the ground, the walls, the mosques and the palaces destroyed. Others thought that Delhi should be left to decay of itself, and that the refugees should be prevented from returning. At first Wilson was ordered to destroy all the fortifications, including the Red Fort and the Selimgarh, but to leave mosques, temples and churches. But he appealed to Lord Canning, pointing out that this would leave the city at the mercy of the Goojurs and the badmashes. And here, for once, Wilson won his case. The Mogul capital was to stand, and gradually those who had fled in the dark September days would trickle back through the gates.

Bahadur Shah Zafar, former King of Delhi and twenty-second of the Moguls, was to be put on trial. In the days before he was arraigned Mrs Hodson visited Begum Zinat Mahal. Even in captivity Zinat Mahal behaved as an empress. Mrs

Hodson was graciously bidden to sit, but, doubting the cleanliness of the charpoy in the Begum's dingy room, she remained standing, a breach of etiquette. The King, however, was insisting on nothing: he slept on his charpoy, retched into his bowl, scratched some verses on the wall with a burnt stick, sat cross-legged fumbling with his worry beads, and remained unperturbed at the stares of the curious who filed through his little room. When a translation of the indictment was handed to him on 5 January he hardly seemed to take in the enormity of the charges.

Bahadur Shah was indicted under four counts. The first was aiding and abetting Bakht Khan, and the second aiding and abetting Mirza Mogul in the seizing of Delhi and the mutiny of the sepoys. The third was that he had levied war against the 'paramount power', in defiance of the agreements that had been made in 1803. The fourth was the only charge that was of real moment and around which his trial was to revolve, that he had been an accessory before and after the fact to the murder of the Christians on 16 May. The court was a court-martial, set up by a special commission from the Governor-General. The president was Colonel Dawes of the Horse Artillery – hastily appointed in place of Brigadier Showers who had commanded an infantry brigade at the battle for Badli-ke-Serai, and was now posted out of Delhi. The other four members of the court were officers from the 60th Rifles, the 61st of Foot, the 6th Carabineers and the 4th Sikh Infantry. The prosecutor was the Deputy Advocate-General, Major Harriot; there was a court interpreter, an insignificant little Eurasian called James Murphy; and the King had his own counsel, a scribe from his own court, Gulam Abas.

At half-past noon on the morning of 27 January – late because at the last minute Brigadier Showers had had to be replaced – the court began its sittings. Every courtesy was accorded to the prisoner. As he shuffled into the Diwan-i-Khas leaning on a stick, between his youngest and favourite son Jawan Bakht Mirza and Gulam Abas, he saw that a couch with piles of cushions had been prepared for him below the dais on which his judges sat. In deference to the prisoner's age the hours of sittings were to be short: the court would not meet until 11 o'clock in the morning and would adjourn at 4 o'clock in the afternoon.

The King seemed to find the proceedings boring. Often he dozed on his pillows, while his son Jawan Bakht 'laughed and chatted with his father's attendants without appearing at all embarrassed.' Later this indecorous behaviour led to Jawan Bakht's being excluded from the hall of public audience. While evidence was being given the King, it was reported, would sometimes 'coil himself up in his shawls, and reclining on the cushions placed for his convenience, would appear perfectly indifferent to the proceedings around him.' Sometimes he would fidget with his rosary of worry beads, or amuse himself by twisting a scarf around his head like a playful child. 'Occasionally, however,' wrote an observer, 'when some particular passage was read, the dull eye would light up, and the bowed head would be raised in marked attention for a few moments – only to relapse into a state of listless indifference.' At times he proclaimed his complete innocence of all the charges; at others he would interrupt with an irrelevant question – once, for instance, asking if the Persians were the same as the Russians.

The laborious proceedings began with a speech from the prosecutor. Some of the rules of evidence, he said, were to be dispensed with. There had been no way of authenticating many of the documents which would be produced, and some of the evidence would be hearsay. It was no ordinary court, but a special commission. Furthermore in one particular the court was limited in its powers. If the King were found guilty it could not pass a death sentence, even for the murders of 16 May. Hodson had given the King the promise that his life would be spared, and this promise Lord Canning said he would honour.

The first days of the trial were spent in the reading of translations of proclamations and petitions, which was intended to establish that the King had been generally recognized and accepted in Delhi as the leader of the revolt. In evidence was a selection of the stream of letters that he had sent to Mirza Mogul, letters from householders and shopkeepers to 'the centre of the world' and 'the protector of the poor' imploring his help against the plunderers from the bahadshi. There was a directive from the King and the court of administration about the raising of money. But much of this evidence tended to show that the King was not the leader and inspiration of rebellion; often he was, rather petulantly, intervening to restrain the excesses of his own soldiery, or to curb the animosity of Moslem towards Hindu.

Several gave evidence about Bahadur Shah's complicity in the murders of Jennings, Douglas and Miss Clifford and the massacre of the Christians in the courtyard. The prosecution attempted to show that the murders had been committed by members of the King's personal bodyguard and even if they had not been acting under the King's orders, the murderers could have been, but were not, restrained by his intervention. Both Chuni Lal, a reporter, and Gulab, one of Mukundlal's messengers, said that they had heard in the city three or four days before the 16th that a massacre of the Christians had been planned and would take place. They had both gone to the courtyard at about 10 o'clock in the morning of that day and had seen the prisoners; Gulab said that they were sitting in rows with their hands bound; Chuni Lal estimated that the murder squad was between a hundred and a hundred and fifty men. Two of the princes had watched from behind the lattices of an upstairs window overlooking the courtyard.

Ahsan Ullah Khan's evidence was neutral. He claimed that it was not common knowledge in the city who had murdered Jennings, but was forced to admit that not one of the King's servants or guards had been punished or dismissed as a result of the murders. When he gave his evidence the hakim never once looked towards the King who sat among his cushions and was, for once, attentive.

Jat Mall's evidence was more favourable. He had seen the

massacre, and claimed that the sepoys had been stirred up by a fanatic, Basant Ali Khan, and that the King had been powerless to restrain them. Jat Mall was the only witness whom Bahadur Shah cross-examined. 'I heard in the city that the King did wish to save the Europeans, particularly the women and children, but that he was overruled by the violence of the soldiers, and had not the firmness to oppose them.' But then, in answer to a question from Colonel Dawes, he admitted that there was room in the palace to hide five hundred.

Then came the evidence of Mrs Aldwell, a Eurasian, the most lengthy and crucial of the trial. On the 11th she and her household had barricaded themselves indoors. She had heard the explosion at the magazine, the sounds of riot and the looting of the houses. In the evening she sent a petition to the King claiming to be a Kashmiri and a Moslem. The guards seem to have believed her, for they ate and drank with her. She escaped the massacre but was later brought before Mirza Mogul, was accused of being a Christian in disguise and condemned to death. She was rescued by the sepoys of the 38th Native Infantry, and sheltered in what had been Captain Douglas' quarters at the Lahore Gate until after the battle of the Hindun River. Mrs Aldwell agreed with all the witnesses that most of those killed had been women and children, that the princes, if not the King, had been spectators, that the pathetic party had been confined for five days in a cramped and airless dungeon in the palace, and that when they were taken to execution they had been told that they were being removed to pleasanter quarters.

What did it all amount to as proof of the King's complicity? There were, according to some but not all the witnesses, members of the King's bodyguard among the murderers. There was a salute of guns fired from the Selimgarh Fort immediately after the massacre, presumably in celebration. One witness said that Basant Ali Khan emerged from the King's apartments before he urged the sepoys to kill. The King in his defence pleaded simply that the killing was done

Above Metcalfe's house and (*below*) Hindu Rao's house immediately after the siege.

Above St James's Church, Delhi, after the siege.
Below John Nicholson's tomb outside the Delhi walls, as photographed by a contemporary.

against his wishes – after all had he not tried to save Captain Douglas, and after he was killed ordered that the body be found for Christian burial? In his remarks to the court Bahadur Shah went over, once again, the old grievances. He talked much about etiquette and the boorishness of many of the bahadshi, presumably to emphasize that he was powerless to control them: 'they used to walk into the Diwan-i-Khas and Hall of Devotion with their shoes on.' But he blamed no other person – not the shahzadas, nor Basant Ali Khan. His soldiers, he thought, had simply 'given themselves up to the devil'.

On 29 March the court convened for the last time. The King was found guilty of all the four charges and sentenced to life imprisonment. After his conviction Bahadur Shah was visited by Austen Layard, traveller, archaeologist and M.P. On his return to London Layard spoke at a public meeting about the King's condition, ill-fed and diseased. But Layard's accusations were strongly denied by the authorities: the King was receiving the best treatment for his unpleasant skin disease; his diet was supervised by a doctor. In the summer the last of the Moguls was moved to Rangoon, where, at the age of eighty-seven, he died.

In the new year of 1858 the refugees began to trickle slowly back into Delhi. Only the Calcutta, Kashmir and Lahore Gates were open. The others were still blocked with rubble and masonry. On presentation of 1 rupee and 2 annas at the Kotwali a charpoy and two stones for the grinding of grain were issued. A Fusilier band began to play daily in front of the battered church of St. James. A traveller reported that by January there was a great deal of traffic once again on the Grand Trunk Road – daks, gharries and camels, burdened and unburdened. In the spring the *Times* correspondent, William Howard Russell, crossed the bridge of boats: it was busy, with room for two lanes of traffic and the street lamps at intervals in working order. He was to spend a 'most civilised evening' with the hospitable Civil Commissioner. The ancient capital, which a few months before had been littered with the bodies of men and animals, was returning to normal.

When Roberts had ridden out of Delhi four days after the fall of the palace across that same bridge of boats the scene had been very different. 'Here a dog gnawed at an uncovered limb; there a vulture, disturbed by our approach from its loathsome meal, but too completely gorged to fly, fluttered away to a safer distance.' Charles Ball, leaving the city in the other direction, said that from the Lahore Gate to Sabsi Mandi, travelling along the road to Kurnal, there was 'an almost continuous line of carcasses of camels, horses and bullocks, with their skins dried into parchment over the sapless bones.' All this had been the debris left behind by siege, assault and capture, 'that wild, exciting, lawless scene – the finale of a long and slow process . . .'

The capture of the city was at first disbelieved by many in the villages surrounding Delhi. Some thought, as Rice Holmes put it, that the salutes from guns and the illuminations were simply 'the last desperate device by which the Feringis hoped to make it appear that they had recovered their ascendancy.' But the ascendancy was not yet fully recovered. There were still many pockets of mutineers from the northern parts of the Punjab to the heart of Bengal.

What had been done was to strike a blow at the heart of the revolt and to remove the national symbol, however tarnished, of the emperor. Now the victors could fan out into the Doab and Rohilkand; they could relieve the provincial capital at Agra, where the Europeans were defending the great fort across the river from the Taj Mahal; and then they could mass for the final relief of Lucknow. After this there would remain only small bands of mutineers to be pursued and captured in the rain-drenched forests of central India.

All this was directed by a new Commander-in-Chief, a man of very different stamp from Anson. Sir Colin Campbell had served in the British army for nearly half a century. He had taken part in the ill-fated Walcheren expedition, at the storming of San Sebastian in the Peninsula, in the war against the Americans in 1814 and against the Chinese in 1842. He had fought against the Sikhs at Chillianwalla and commanded the Highland Division at the battle of the Alma in the Crimea. There was no officer in the Queen's service with a greater experience of war than this lean Scot with grey curly hair, whose origins were humble, whose methods were precise and sure. Perhaps, as Rice Holmes wrote of him, he was not a 'heaven-born general', was not 'a scholar in the art of war like Havelock' and had not the dash and intuition that were Nicholson's, but he stands out as the only truly great general of the highest rank in the dark period in the army's history that separates the age of Wellington from the age of Wolseley.

It was Campbell who was Commander-in-Chief in India when the reconstruction of the sepoy army began. As a result of the events of 1857 and 1858 the old Bengal army came to an end. All of the ten regiments of cavalry had mutinied and sixty-one of the seventy-four battalions of infantry. Even some of the irregulars had had to be disarmed to prevent them going over to the mutineers. In general it was the newer regiments in the Company's service which had remained true to their salt – all the Sikhs, for instance, with the exception of the possibly mishandled Ludhiana Regiment who joined the Lucknow rebels. The most disaffected had been sepoys recruited from Oudh; the most loyal those from the Punjab.

There were to be two sweeping changes in the Indian Army after the mutiny. The first was a change in areas of recruitment. The numbers of the 'purbiah', soldiers recruited from the Gangetic plain, were to be reduced. They had been the first to rebel. Moreover their reputation as soldiers had suffered in the campaigns against Afghans and Sikhs during the twenty years or so before the mutiny. Increasingly the purbiahs were to make way for the Sikhs, the Punjabis and the Gurkhas who had proved their worth and their loyalty on the ridge and the walls of Delhi.

Second, there was to be a new type of organization. The emphasis was to shift from the old 'regular' regiments. The old List of the Bengal regiments was rearranged: all regiments from Oudh were disbanded, and there was little more recruiting from that area of disaffection. The emphasis in later Victorian India was to be on 'irregular' contingents. In these there were to be small cadres of British officers. The commanders would be given lump sums to raise, clothe and mount their units. There would be more Indian officers, and these promoted at a younger age; by the turn of the century young Indians of good family were being trained at Sandhurst. Most important of all the Native Artillery was to come to an end. No longer was the sepoy army to be a copy of the British. The shako and the cross-belt were discarded in the new regiments, Coke's Rifles, Wilde's Rifles, Hodson's Horse and Probyn's Horse.

The system was to filter to the armies of the south, and only the Madras Light Cavalry was to remain mounted by the Government – all others would be mounted from inclusive rates of pay. The new regiments would be more mobile and, while remaining what Indian regiments had always been, mercenaries, would be more closely knit together. They would prove more suitable than the old army of the Company for the small-scale wars and the campaigns on the frontier. The emerging Indian Army of the 1860s and 1870s was itself, perhaps, a posthumous victory for Hodson and Nicholson.

Old abuses and causes of complaint, too, were to disappear. In the generation before the mutiny too many of the most talented officers had been removed from their regiments for 'civilian' service. Now, with the arrival of more and more of the 'competition wallahs' the Indian Civil Service was to be strengthened, and officers of merit would remain where they belonged, in their regiments. The Gladstone reforms in civil and military administration would be echoed in the Indian Empire. Paradoxically, the more 'irregular' the Indian Army became, the more professional it was.

On 1 November in all stations in India the Queen's Proclamation was read to the accompaniment of parades, fireworks, artillery salutes, banquets and religious services.

All political parties in England were agreed that the blame for the mutiny lay with the Honourable East India Company, and that its rule should come to an end. The Queen became in fact, though not yet in name, Empress of India, and Lord Canning, the last Governor-General, became the first Viceroy. All those who held offices under the Company should continue to hold them under the Crown. All the Company's treaties with the princes should be honoured by the Crown. There should be no extension of British territory in India. There should be religious freedom, and the customs and usages of the Queen's new subjects should be respected.

Above all, an amnesty was proclaimed. It applied to all uncaptured mutineers, except those who had been guilty of the murder of Europeans. But even by the time of the Proclamation and amnesty, the sepoy war had not yet run its course. There was still to be the winter campaign in Oudh, the operations against the uncaptured in the centre and the long pursuit and eventual execution of the mutineers' leader there, Tantia Topi.

Less than twenty years after the storming of Delhi Major-General Upton of the United States Army was to eulogize the armies of India. 'The military institutions of India present more features for our imitation than those of any army or country in Europe,' he wrote. 'The value and economy of native troops were early discovered, and nowhere in history has the wisdom of a government been so signally rewarded as in the organization of the native army.' At first it seems a strange choice for such fulsome praise. It was only six years before the General wrote this that the armies of Bismarck had encircled and defeated the marshals of France and their emperor with organization, weapons and deployment superior to any that had been seen in the history of the world. The German was a national army; at its heart was a general staff chosen from the ablest in Prussia, reared on the wisdom of Clausewitz and Frederick the Great; to support it was the transport and machinery of the age of steam and electricity.

There were in fact few points of comparison between the armies of a nation-state in Europe and those of the Indian Empire. At the time of the mutiny there were in India three armies; and these remained after the reconstruction as distinct as they had been before 'the Devil's Wind', as the Indians described the mutiny, blew across the dusty plains of the north. Their traditions and their ways of life were different. The mutiny hardly found an echo in the Madras army in the south. The Bombay army, though it poached on the recruiting grounds of the mutinous Bengal army, remained by and large true to its salt.

It was not only among the sepoys that the ways of life had been so different between the north, south and west. By the 1850s the European officers of the Bengal army were a special breed. They were close to the centre of power at Calcutta. There were chances of political promotion outside their regiments greater than in Madras or Bombay. Some lived in greater style, a style very different from that of the ascetic men who had raised their regiments at the turn of the century, and those that were raising new ones near the north-west frontier. 'I saw a captain of the Bengal army,' wrote a German observer on the eve of the mutiny, 'on his way to the army of reserve at Ferozpur, with two large waggons drawn by oxen full of geese, fowls, pigeons, wines, sugar, coffee, tea, and numberless tin cases of delicacies to say nothing of the goats, sheep and the camels which carried his tent.' It was claimed that, while in Bombay and Madras the sepoys became 'half-European', in the north the officers became 'half-Hindu', and paid so much attention to caste and status that they 'lost their sense of professional soldiership and discipline'.

Out of the mutiny a new doctrine was to emerge. It was one that fitted well with the climate of thought that was partly created by, and partly reflected in, Darwin's *Origin of Species*. Lord Salisbury could refer to the 'active' and 'passive' races in the world; and Sir Henry Lawrence writing on the eve of the mutiny could observe that 'once two Roman legions held Britain; now as many Britons might hold Italy.' Might not there be 'active' and 'passive' races in the sub-continent of India as there were in the continent of Europe?

The history of the mutiny suggested to many that there were; the fighting qualities of Punjabi and Sikh had appeared to be superior to those of the purbiah from Oudh and the brahmin of the Gangetic plain. Above all, the Gurkha hillmen from Nepal, unencumbered by caste and taboo, might provide a mercenary army for the British Empire in the nineteenth century as once another mountain people, the Swiss, had provided one for the royal houses of Valois, Habsburg and Bourbon. Or might there not be some strange affinity between the highlanders from the Grampians who marched with their bagpipes into Lucknow, and the highlanders from the Himalayas who had defended, unrelieved, Hindu Rao's house on the ridge through that terrible summer of 1857?

Some thought that the determinants were blood, breeding and geography: these were the factors that made a race active or passive, warlike or non-warlike. And so there evolved the notion of the 'martial races'. An exponent of this was Lord Roberts of Kandahar who thought there was yet another factor, history. When he became Commander-in-Chief of the army in the south he used to make tours of inspection during the cold season to discover 'the needs and capabilities of the men of the Madras army'. This is how he described what he did on these expeditions: 'I tried hard to discover in them those fighting qualities which had distinguished their forefathers during the wars of the last and the beginning of the present century. But long years of peace, and the security and prosperity attending it, had evidently had upon them, as they always seem to have on Asiatics, a softening and deteriorating effect . . .' And he had no patience with those of his superiors who held the 'erroneous belief that one native was as good as another for purposes of war.'

Half a century after the mutiny similar views were expressed by another Commander-in-Chief in India, General Sir O'Moore Creagh. 'In the hot, flat regions,' he wrote, 'are found races, timid both by religion and habit, servile to their superiors, but tyrannical to their inferiors, and quite unwarlike. In other parts where the winter is cold, the warlike minority is to be found. Nowhere,' he added pessimistically, 'are they the equal in that respect to Europeans or Japanese.' In other words, those whose winter climate was the winter climate of Britain would be found most suitable for the service of the Raj; these were the Gurkhas and frontier dwellers.

Immediately after the mutiny a commission was set up to enquire into the organization of the Indian Army. The chairman was General Peel who was then Secretary of State for War: but in that office, in the days of the unreformed army, he had had little or no say in matters concerning the sepoys. The commission included the Duke of Cambridge who had been a distinguished divisional commander in the Crimea and Lord Stanley who was later to be Secretary of State for India. It took a mass of evidence and produced a lengthy report.

The commission heard evidence and suggestions about recruitment. Some witnesses, generally those familiar with the Bombay and Madras armies, wanted a balanced recruitment, drawing on all sections of society within an area. Birth and origins should not, they felt, be the important factors, but individual suitability. Foremost among these was Sir Bartle Frere, Commissioner and later Governor of Sind. Others wanted the proscription from the armies of certain castes and races. A general of great experience, Hearsey, who had commanded at Barrackpore when Mangal Pandy first defied the Raj, was the exponent of this. Whole areas of the subcontinent, he thought, should be blacklisted – Oudh, the Doab and Rohilkand; and so too should certain classes – all Brahmins and Moslems from 'Hindustan', by which he really meant the Gangetic plain. Caste had no place in an army. 'Any soldier refusing to work because it interfered with his caste,' he stated, 'was to be tried by court-martial and sentenced to be flogged, or transportation for life.' Might it not be expedient, thought Hearsey, to recruit from outside India, among Malays, Chinese and even South American Christians?

Sir John Lawrence, Neville Chamberlain and Sir Herbert Edwardes took up a position between these two extremes. They agreed with Sir Bartle Frere that individual suitability should be the criterion, and this should not preclude recruits even from the areas that had been most disaffected. They wanted to spread the net wider, to include not only Punjabis but Eurasians. They considered that the more groups that were included within the army, the more race would counterbalance race and caste counterbalance caste. In the end the commission recommended that 'the Native Army should be composed of different nationalities and castes, and as a general rule, mixed promiscuously through each regiment.'

This differed materially from the report of those who had served in the Punjab. To make the native army of India safe it was first necessary to have the counterpoise of a large enough European army and next, they thought, 'comes the counterpoise of Natives against Natives.' Might it not be a wise practice 'to mix up all available military races of India in each and every regiment?' It was a solution at first sight attractive, but the Punjab officers rejected it as 'it is found that different races mixed together do not long preserve their distinctiveness; their corners and angles, and feeling, and prejudices get rubbed off, till at last they assimilate, and the object of their association to a considerable extent is lost.' It was important to preserve the distinctiveness, the fear that one Moslem had for another: corps should be provincial, and national rivalries should be fostered. As far as possible locally-raised regiments should be used for local purposes. Much of the trouble had started when the soldiers of Hindustan had marched into the lands of the north-west. By what might be called the provincial system, the Punjab committee thought that 'two great evils are avoided, firstly, that community of feeling throughout the Native Army, and that mischievous political activity and intrigue which results from association with other races and travel in other Indian provinces; and secondly, that through discontent and alienation from the service which has undoubtedly sprung up since extended conquest has carried our Hindustani soldiers so far from their homes in India proper.'

The reforms, of course applied mainly to the Bengal army; the conditions that made the reforms necessary had not really pertained in the armies of the other two presidencies. In the event, by 1864, the Bengal army was to have twenty 'mixed' regiments, sixteen partially 'mixed' but with companies composed of homogenous ethnic groups, and only seven drawn solely from one race, Sikhs and Gurkhas. Furthermore, sepoys were rarely to serve outside the presidencies in which they had been recruited.

In the years after the storming of the walls of Delhi a new army was slowly built up in India. The centres of recruitment shifted, the dangerous tensions in the old purbiah regiments were relieved, 'irregular' corps grew at the expense of the 'regular', and new races increasingly enlisted, Sikhs, Pathans and Gurkhas. So too did the position of the sepoys change. Opportunities for promotion within the regiment – but not beyond it – were greatly increased. In the pre-mutiny regiments of the Bengal army promotion to commissioned ranks among the sepoys had been strictly according to seniority, the gerontocracy that was a feature of the army as a whole being too often mirrored in the regiment. One colonel had tried to depart from the practice and declined to promote a havildar on the grounds of senility: when the news was broken to the havildar he had a heart attack.

A new system of granting Viceroy's Commissions was to become universal. Talent and seniority were to be balanced in the selection. The methods were to vary significantly between different types of regiment. In those such as the Gurkhas and the Sikhs it was straightforward. But in regiments known as 'class company regiments' – that is, partially mixed, but where each company was composed exclusively of one race – promotion could only go to a sepoy of the race in which the vacancy occurred. This ensured a unique structure in regiments of the new Indian Army. General control of a regiment remained in the hands of a few British officers, just as control of the whole army did through an entirely British staff. Between himself and the British officers the sepoy had, however, an officer of his own race and background promoted, largely through merit, from the ranks: the jemadar, subadar, and subadar-major were in no sense non-commissioned officers, and were to share the duties of those who came from Sandhurst.

Armies should reflect the structure of the society from which they spring. The more complex the structure, the more complex the organization needs to be if the bonds of loyalty and discipline are to remain intact. This lesson was taught by the mutiny. It was learnt, and out of the fires of Cawnpore, Lucknow and Delhi was to grow that army which General Upton considered to be beyond compare.

With all this came, sometimes, a new partisanship on the part of the British officers. To be effective they had to understand the nuances of class and sub-class among the Indians they recruited and led. Many of them, as a Gurkha officer pointed out, 'suffered a kind of conversion', and began to see many things as their men saw them. There was the feeling that one martial race had an affinity with another, that the British officer in some ways had more in common with those whom he led than with the non-martial of his own kind. In the days of Clive and Hastings there had been a social equality between the Indians of the higher social classes and British officers and administrators. The gulf between them appeared in the thirty years or so before the mutiny. It was to begin to be bridged in the generation that followed. Once again the British officer was to make his home in the regiment, and was to identify with some of the customs of the particular race of which he felt himself, in a sense, a part. These customs were fostered, and sometimes given a regimental slant: weapons were blessed by the maulvis, gurus and pundits of the regiment, and British officers often joined in these ceremonies naturally and unself-consciously. As the British officers were sharing more in the culture of the sepoys, so too did the sepoys absorb some of the notions of the armies of Europe: the idea of allegiance was gradually to replace the idea of being true to the salt.

Perhaps there need never have been a siege of Delhi. It has been suggested that the general whose vacillation and inactivity were most culpable was not Sir Archdale Wilson, but General Hewitt. When the mutineers at Meerut left for Delhi on the evening of 10 May they did so as a disorganized mob, and they seem to have left on a sudden impulse, as much to escape immediate retribution as to capture what had once been the capital of an empire. A squadron of carabineers was available for pursuit. There was a strong battery of horse artillery, and there were the 60th Rifles unengaged in the garrison. Moreover the parties of mutineers made no forced march on Delhi; many loitered behind and some dropped out. One captain of the carabineers volunteered to lead a pursuing expedition of his own men with a troop of horse artillery and some of the 60th. His plan was to intercept the mutineers at the bridge over the Hindun river. This would have been by no means an impossible feat; a few days later two subalterns carrying despatches with a small escort travelled one hundred and thirty miles on unbroken horses. But the plan, thought Hewitt, 'was too hazardous'. Hugh Gough, musing on it all years later, thought that 'even if the mutineers had arrived before the pursuing force, I believe the moral effect of the approach of the British troopers would have deterred the Native Infantry from breaking out, and Delhi would have been saved.'

Strangely no less a person than Frederick Roberts was to justify the inactivity of Hewitt. He alone among the major writers of eye-witness accounts thought that pursuit on 10 May would have been useless. British infantry, the 60th Rifles, could not, he thought, have reached Delhi until the following evening. 'Only a very few European cavalry,' he wrote, 'were available for pursuit, for the carabineers were mainly recruits still in the riding school, and their horses for the most part were quite unbroken.' The mutineers would have had a considerable start and their cavalry could not have been overtaken; and their infantry 'would have scattered over the country, and favoured by the darkness have defied pursuit.' This was a generous but probably misguided defence of Hewitt. If Roberts himself had been in command at Meerut on that fateful evening, would there have been any question of allowing the 3rd Cavalry to reach the gates of Delhi without an attempt of any kind to pursue and intercept them on their way? One officer commented tersely that 'one hundred and fifty mounted riflemen could have saved the city that night.' They were available but not forthcoming.

Two wars of mid-Victorian England were fought, for the first time, under the glare of publicity. One was the war in the Crimea and the other the mutiny in India. These were the first major military undertakings since the invention of the electric telegraph and one at least was observed and reported upon by the ablest journalist of his day, William Howard Russell of *The Times*. Both wars uncovered for the British people things, good and bad, that had been unknown or only vaguely felt: the deep reservoirs of heroism in a common soldiery recruited for the most part from the lowest orders in society, defects among many of their leaders. Both wars led to reforms that were to last for a century or so: the abolition of purchase of commissions and the professionalization of the British army that began with Cardwell, the reconstruction of the Indian army that began with Campbell. Both wars roused a peculiar passion among the English people.

England applauded the invasion of the Crimea; and Tennyson in his sure voice, one who always 'held the right opinions for the time of year', trumpeted his pleasure: 'the peace that I deemed no peace was over and done.' Those who deplored the expedition were reviled. John Bright had been the hero of working men in the north – but in 1855 as the leader of a peace party, this 'broad-brimmed hawker of holy things' was burnt in effigy in Sheffield. So too, when news of the fires at Meerut, the murders in the palace courtyard at Delhi, the well full of corpses at Cawnpore and the carnage at Lucknow was brought to the English people, a nation was banded together for one purpose. From June to October *Punch* printed the weekly cartoons – of Britannia with her sword defending the defenceless, of the lion leaping on the Bengal tiger. Disraeli pleaded for moderation, and was cartooned as the rebels' camp-follower preparing their curry. Cardinal Wiseman at first condemned the mutineers as beasts of the jungle, and then began to deplore the blood-lust of his own people: week after week he was lampooned in *Punch* and burnt in effigy as he had been six years before, when the establishment of the Catholic hierarchy had offended popular Protestant opinion.

Editors of the more popular papers knew what was wanted. 'We mentioned yesterday, in anticipation of the next telegram of Indian news, the halt which General Havelock has made in his second march upon Lucknow, and the probability that, by this time, Sepoy avengement may have committed a terrible crime in that city,' ran an item in the *Morning Star* in October 1857. 'We hope, most sincerely, that we are not wrong in further anticipating that we shall, within the next two months, hear of many additional horrors that have been perpetrated.' *The Times*, quite simply, wanted every mutineer put to death: 'every tree and gable-end in the place should have its burden in the shape of a mutineer's carcase.' So did a speaker at the Oxford Union: when the ground in front of every cannon was strewn with the bones of the rebels 'then talk of mercy. Then you may find some to listen.' The crimes of the mutineers, declared Lord Palmerston with relish, were 'such as to be imagined and perpetrated only by demons sallying forth from the lowest depths of hell.' An officer complacently remarked of the capture of Cawnpore that 'no maudlin clemency was to mark the fall of the city.'

But it was not horrors only that the people wanted; they wanted heroes as well. The showering of praise was often as indiscriminate as the cry for vengeance. Wilson, the croaking obstructive, was fêted as Lord Cardigan had been, when Nicholson with his dark and terrifying courage was under the stone slab near the Kashmir Gate, and Hodson – no less a hero because he was also a cad – had choked in his own blood at the Begum Kothi. These were the real heroes. Roberts in a long and wholly creditable life remembered Nicholson as the most inspiring commander he had served under, and the bravest. Death must have been almost a relief to Hodson as his deceit and chicanery increasingly caught up with him.

There were other heroes on the ridge whose deeds were unsung. Baird Smith battled with pain and illness greater than Wilson's, and which were to kill him at an early age. Yet for weeks, with his wounds untended, he limped around the camp sharing his own particular calmness and confidence with the exhausted engineers and gunners. Neville Chamberlain, severely wounded, was carried in a doolie from the ridge to check the rout after the reverses of Major Reid's column; this, perhaps, was the decisive action on 14 September. There were no Victoria Crosses for Hodson, Baird Smith and Chamberlain: for Nicholson there was a memorial slab in Delhi, an equestrian statue in Ireland and a street named after him off the Blackfriars Road.

In the 1850s the Empire, apart from India, was small. It was not until the 1880s and 1890s that the British were to make the great inroads into 'the dark places of this globe', pressing downwards from Egypt into the Sudan and Uganda, upwards from the coasts of southern Africa into Rhodesia, outwards from Pegu to Mandalay. But the crisis of empire had already been faced on the walls of Delhi and the narrow lanes that lay behind them. Here were fought the battles which Sir Charles Crosthwaite, the Anglo-Indian historian, aptly called 'the epic of the Race'.

Chronology of Main Events

23 April 1857	Refusal of the skirmishers of the 3rd Cavalry at Meerut to accept the new cartridges.
9 May	Sentencing of the Meerut mutineers.
10 May	Rising of the 3rd Cavalry at Meerut.
11 May	Fall of Delhi to the mutineers.
13 May	Disarming of mutineers at Mian-Mir.
30 May	Battle of the Hindun river.
8 June	Battle of Badli-ke-Serai. Occupation of the ridge.
23 June	Centenary of Plassey. Mutineers assault the British position.
24 June	Arrival of Neville Chamberlain and Baird Smith in the British camp.
2 July	Mutineers reinforced. Bakht Khan commander of the King's army.
5 July	Death of General Barnard.
12 July	Battle of the Ravi river.
17 July	Archdale Wilson commander of the Delhi Field Force.
24 July	Nicholson and the Movable Column march for Delhi.
7 August	Arrival of Nicholson on the ridge.
25 August	Battle of Najafgarh Jheel.
4 September	Arrival of the siege-train.

8 September	The artillery barrage begins.
14 September	Assault of the four columns on the walls. The wounding of Nicholson.
15 September	Penetration of the city and the soldiers' debauch.
20 September	Capture of the Lahore Gate, Jumma Masjid and the Red Fort.
21 September	The King surrenders to Hodson.
22 September	Hodson shoots the three princes.
23 September	Death of Nicholson.
January 1858	Trial and sentencing of the King of Delhi.

Bibliography of works consulted

ANSON, Octavius: With H.M. 9th Lancers in the Indian Mutiny (1896)

BALL, Charles: History of the Indian Mutiny (2 vols) (1858)

BAYLEY, John: The Assault of Delhi (1876)

BOURCHIER, Col. George: Eight months Campaign against the Bengal Sepoy Army (1857)

Cambridge History of India

CAVE-BROWNE, Rev. J: The Punjab and Delhi in 1857 (2 vols) (1861)

CHATTOPADHYAYA, H: The Sepoy Rebellion of 1857, A Social Study and Analysis (1957)

CHAUDHURI, S.B: Civil Rebellion in the Indian Mutinies (1957)

CHAUDHURI, S.B: Theories of the Indian Mutiny (1965)

COHEN, Stephen P: The Indian Army, its Contribution to the Development of a Nation (1971)

COLLIER, Richard: The Sound of Fury (1963)

CORK, Barry J: Rider on a Grey Horse (biography of Hodson) (1958)

DALY, Henry: Memoirs of Gen. Sir Henry Dermot Daly (1905)

Dictionary of National Biography

EDWARDES, Michael: The Necessary Hell (1958)

EDWARDES, Michael: The Orchid House (1960)

EDWARDES, Michael: Red Year (1972)

FORBES-MITCHELL, Sergeant William: Reminiscences of the Great Mutiny (1893)
FORREST, Gen. Sir George: History of the Indian Mutiny (1904)
FORTESCUE, Hon. J.W: History of the British Army, Vol. XIII (1930)
GOUGH, Gen. Sir Hugh, V.C: Old Memories (1897)
GREATHED, Hervey: Letters written during the Siege of Delhi (1857)
GRIFFITHS, Capt. Charles: A Narrative of the Siege of Delhi (ed. 1930)
History of the Sirmoor Battalion (2 vols) (privately circulated)
HODSON, Rev. George (editor): Twelve Years of a Soldier's Life, or Hodson of Hodson's Horse (1883)
HOLMES, T. Rice: History of the Indian Mutiny (1898)
HUSAIN, A.M: Bahadur Shah 11 (1958)
INNES, J. McLeod: The Sepoy Revolt (1897)
IRELAND, William: A History of the Siege of Delhi by an Officer who served there (1861)
KAYE, Sir John: History of the Sepoy War (1864)
KAYE, Sir John, and Malleson, Col. H: The Indian Mutiny (6 vols) (1888)
KHOSLA, G.D: Bahadur Shah 11 (1969)
LEASOR, James: The Red Fort (1956)
MACKENZIE, Col. A.R.D: Mutiny Memoirs. (1891)
MACLAGAN, Michael: 'Clemency' Canning (1962)
MACMUNN, Lt. Gen. Sir George: The Indian Mutiny in Perspective (1931)
MAJUMDAR, R.C: The Sepoy Mutiny and Revolt of 1857 (1957)
MASON, Philip: A Matter of Honour (1974)
MAUNSELL, F.R: The Siege of Delhi (1912)
MEDLEY, Julius: A Year's Campaigning in India (1858)
METCALF, T.R: Aftermath of Revolt, India 1857–1870 (1965)
METCALFE, Sir Theophilus (translator): Two Native

Narratives of the Indian Mutiny (1898)
MORRIS, James: By Heaven's Command. (1973)
MUIR, Sir William: Report of the Intelligence Department of the North-West Provinces (1902)
MUTER, Mrs Dunbar: My Recollections of the Sepoy Revolt. (1911)
NORMAN, Major H.W: A Narrative of the Campaign of the Delhi Mutiny (1858)
ORLICH, Leopold von: The Military Mutiny in India (1858)
PEARSON, Hesketh: The Hero of Delhi [Nicholson] (1939)
ROBERTS, Frederick Sleigh, V.C., (later Earl Roberts): Forty-one Years in India. (1897)
ROBERTS, Frederick Sleigh, V.C. (later Earl Roberts): Letters written during the Indian Mutiny (ed. 1924)
ROTTON, Rev. James: The Chaplain's Narrative of the Siege of Delhi (1858)
RUSSELL, William Howard: My Diary in India 1858–1859 (1860)
SEATON, Thomas: From Cadet to Colonel (1866)
SEN, Surendra Nath: Eighteen-Fifty-Seven (1957)
SHADWELL, Lt. Gen. L: Sir Colin Campbell (2 vols) (1881)
SHERER, J.W: Daily Life during the Indian Mutiny (1898)
SPEAR, Percival: Twilight of the Mughuls (1951)
THACKERAY, Edward, V.C: Two Indian Campaigns in 1857/1858 (1896)
THACKERAY, Edward, V.C: A Subaltern in the Indian Mutiny (letters ed. 1930)
TREVELYAN, G.O: Cawnpore (1865)
TROTTER, Capt. Lionel: Life of John Nicholson (1898)
TROTTER, Capt. Lionel: A Leader of Light Horse (Hodson) (1901)
TURNBULL, Col. J.R: Letters written during the Siege of Delhi (1876)
VIBART, Col. Sir Edward: The Sepoy Mutiny as seen by a Subaltern from Delhi to Lucknow (1898)
VIBART, Col. Henry: Richard Baird Smith, Leader of the Delhi Heroes (1897)

WHEELER, Edmund H: What shall we do at Delhi? (1857)
WILBERFORCE, Reginald: An Unrecorded Chapter in the Indian Mutiny (1894)
WOOD, Sir Evelyn (Field Marshal): The Revolt in Hindustan (1908)
WOODRUFF, Philip: The Men who ruled India (1953)
YOUNG, Col. Keith: Delhi, 1857 (1902)

Index

Index